Walking Caithness and Sutherland

Clan Walk Guides

Walking Caithness and Sutherland

Walking Scotland Series
Volume 18

Mary Welsh
and
Christine Isherwood

First published by Clan Books, 2010

ISBN 978 1873597 34 7
Text and Illustrations
© Mary Welsh
and Christine Isherwood 2010

The authors wish to express their gratitude to
Jennifer Outhwaite, Dr Catherine Isherwood and Tom Welsh
for their help in preparing this volume

Clan Books
Clandon House
The Cross, Doune
Perthshire
FK16 6BE

Printed and bound in Great Britain by
Bell & Bain Ltd., Glasgow

Publisher's Note

Everyone who has explored the two northern-most mainland counties will agree that they each have a special, almost mystical character, perhaps because they stretch so far from the hubs of modern urban living.

The further west you venture from the main communication routes, the winding, narrow "main" roads and the rail line still maintaining its tenuous foothold on an inhospitable track-base, the greater is the sense of wonder at the scale and sheer beauty of these often inaccessible lands.

We offer this new volume, believing it may help readers to discover many of these delights, but must emphasize that some of the routes followed are not trivial strolls but serious expeditions into remote places where poor equipment and heedless timing could be disastrous.

The Authors' Golden Rules for Good, Safe Walking

- Wear suitable clothes and take adequate waterproofs.
- Walk in strong footwear; walking boots are advisable.
- Carry the relevant map and a compass and know how to use them.
- Carry a whistle; remember six long blasts repeated at one minute intervals is the distress signal.
- Do not walk alone, and tell someone where you are going.
- If mist descends, return.
- Keep all dogs under strict control. Observe all "No Dogs" notices – they are there for very good reasons.

In all volumes of the WALKING SCOTLAND series, the authors make every effort to ensure accuracy, but changes can occur after publication. Reports of such changes are welcomed by the publisher. Neither the publisher nor the authors can accept responsibility for errors, omissions or any loss or injury.

Contents

Walk Number		Page Number
Kintail		
1a	Rosehall and the Falls of Achness	7
1b	Raven's Rock Gorge	10
2a	Falls of Shin	12
2b	Ord Hill, Lairg	14
3	Spinningdale and Loch Migdale	16
4	Dornoch to Embo	19
5	Dornoch Point	22
6	Balblair Wood	25
7	Ben Bhraggie and the Big Burn	28
8	Dunrobin and Carn Liath Broch	32
9	Morven	35
10a	Dunbeath Village	38
10b	Dunbeath Archaeological Trail	40
11	Suisgill and the Strath of Kildonan	44
12	Forsinard Flows, the Dubh Lochan Trail	47
13	Rumster Forest	50
14	Munsary	53
15	The South Yarrows Archaeology Trail	56
16	Noss Head and Girnigoe Castle	59
17	Stacks of Duncansby	62
18a	St John's Point and Scotland's Haven	66
18b	Flagstone Trail and Castleton Community Wood	69
19	Strathy Point	72
20	Bettyhill and Creag Ruadh	75
21	Rosal Clearance Township and the King's Stone	78
22	Ben Klibreck	81

Walk Number		Page Number
23	Ben Loyal	84
24	Ben Hope	87
25	The Wheelhouse, Loch Eriboll	90
26	Faraid Head, Durness	93
27	Sandwood Bay	96
28	Polin and Oldshoremore	99
29	Loch na Tuadh, between Arkle and Foinaven	102
30	Handa Island	105
31	Kylestrome and Loch Glendhu	108
32	Eas a'Chual Aluinn	111
33	Spidean Coinich, Quinag	114
34	Drumbeg Peat Roads	117
35	The Old Man of Stoer	120
36	Achmelvich to Alltanabradhan	123
37	River Inver and Glen Canisp	126
38	Falls of Kirkaig and Fionn Loch	129
39a	The Traligill Caves, Inchnadamph	132
39b	The Bone Caves	136
40	Canisp	139

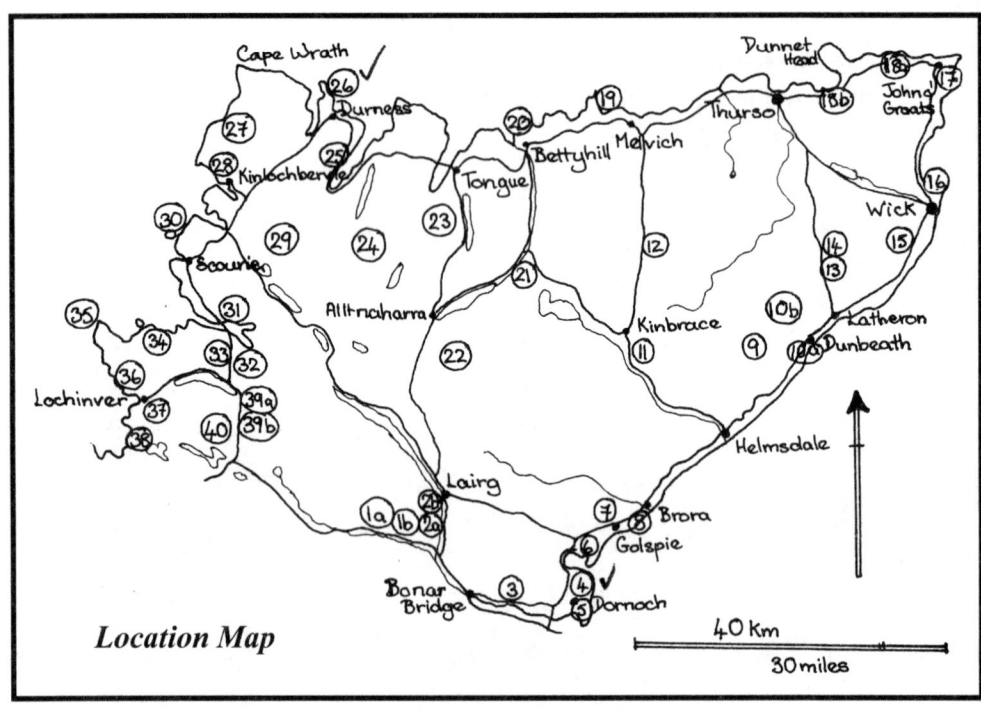

Location Map

1a

Rosehall and the Falls of Achness

Park in the large forestry car park at Rosehall, grid ref 480019. Access this from the A837 Ledmore Junction to Bonar Bridge road, about seven miles east of Oykel Bridge.

Formerly the land was two estates, called Achness and Altas (or Altass). In 1748 it was bought by William Bailley, who renamed it **Rosehall** and began the planting of the forests, which are here today. Rosehall (or Rosshal on early documents) is probably of Norse derivation, meaning horse field.

The Falls of Achness are to be found on the River Cassley which has risen near the west coast on Ben More Assynt. At Achness it flows through a fine gorge in a series of dramatic falls. The lower fall is broken by a high rock apron forming several small falls, which help the salmon to go upstream.

Falls of Achness

1 Visit the log-built centre which has information boards about the forest and the wildlife. Then go to the left of the cabin and take a forest track, through a gate. After ¼ mile/½ km take a well-made, way-marked path on the left which winds down through pleasant open woodland, full of birdsong in spring. Listen for wren, song thrush, chaffinch, and both willow and wood warblers. If you are lucky you may see a small group of crossbills in the tree tops or flying over. Follow the path down to a small gate at the bottom and go out to the minor road, where there is the Millennium Cairn, built by the inhabitants of Rosehall and Invercassley.

2 Turn right along the minor road and walk on past Achness Hotel, then round a curve with woodland to your right and open pastures to your left. A mound in trees across the field is the remains of a broch. Just beyond some animal pens take a reinforced track through a gate on the left and walk down to the river bank, where there is a grassy area used by fishermen for parking. Turn right again here and walk along a broad grassy path, then a smaller path across a gravel bank with an old cemetery on the right and the fine broad river swirling in a pool on the left. Climb stone steps up a steep bank; these may be very slippery after rain and if you are worried about them go round the other side of the graveyard. From the bank at the top of the steps there is a stunning view of the foaming river ahead, full of rapids and falls. Walk on with mature beech trees to the right. There is a bench strategically situated to give a view of the upper falls. Go past this, ignore a path to the right and continue along a small path through a gate. This is a fishermen's path, edging the river which is still full of rapids and very spectacular, and running through open woods of birch and pine with bilberry. Cross a plank over a tiny burn. Soon the path turns away, where the river levels out, and makes for the road again. Cross a stile onto the road and turn right.

3 Walk for 220yds/200m along the road and turn left into forestry at a large deer gate in a parking space; there is a sign welcoming you to Rosehall woods. Wind

Walk 1a

up the good path through open woodland, mainly larch, birch and pine, until you reach a forest track at a T junction. Turn left on the Wild Woods Trail–there are wooden pictures of the animals which live here, and excellent poems written by the local schoolchildren. At a bench turn right onto a path, which climbs at first and then contours along the hillside. Look for pine marten droppings, and cones eaten by red squirrels. Ignore a path off to the right, cross a small burn on a stout wooden bridge and take a path going left which climbs up to a viewpoint. At first the path runs through thick forest but soon reaches yet another seat with a view of a fine waterslide on the small burn. Beyond this cross a bridge over a tributary and zigzag delightfully up through open birch with the main burn (Allt a'Chaorainn), a series of small falls and waterchutes, on the left. Primroses cover the ground in spring, with deep purple violets and wood anemones, and bitter vetch. Soon you reach the top of the wood and a deer fence blocks further progress; here there is another seat and an open area where you can look out above the trees. Beyond the deer fence are old pine trees scattered across the hillside.

Pine marten

4 Return down to the main path and turn left, following waymarks. Contour along the hillside to emerge from the trees above an area of clear-fell, where gorse and broom line the path. Continue into trees again, bearing right at the end where a cycle trail joins the track. Just before you reach a deer gate and some buildings, take a smaller path on the right and walk down through a little gate in the deer fence to reach the car park.

Practicals

Type of walk: A lovely walk through open forest, mainly of birch, scots pine and larch, with a spectacular stretch of the River Cassley as a bonus. The paths are good, well-constructed and well-drained throughout. Very little of the walk is on roads or ordinary forest tracks.

Total distance: 4 miles/6.5km
Time: 2 hours
Maps: OS Explorer 440/Landranger 16

1b

Raven's Rock Gorge

Park in a small car park in the pine forest above the gorge, grid ref 497009. Access this by a narrow lane that leaves the A839 at grid ref 506016.

Tracks and paths meander through woodland composed of mature silver fir, beech and spruce, beside the Allt Mor burn (**Big Burn**) as it passes through the steep-sided Raven's Rock Gorge. Perhaps ravens did live here once. We didn't spot any. Maybe you will be more lucky.

Bear Sculpture, Raven's Rock

1 Walk the descending track from the car park through the pine forest. Ignore a right turn (your return route) and continue down the sloping way through the lovely woodland to come beside the Allt Mor burn.

2 Follow the winding river on a good path into the magical gorge. Admire the wooden sculpture of a bear. The sides of the gorge gradually become steeper and steeper and in many places dense moss carpets the steep slopes, boulders and tree trunks alike, creating a green wonderland. Huge craggy cliffs rear upwards and eventually it is difficult to spot the tops of the trees or glimpse the sky. Exciting boardwalks, stone steps and railed ladders take you over difficult terrain and across small streams heading on to join

the burn. They also provide safe viewpoints from where to enjoy the burn's tumultuous progress. Finally a railed way leads you up to a seat from where you will be awe struck by a spectacular single fall on the burn.

3 Then follow the good track as it leads away from the river through pine forest once more. Pause at a viewpoint to enjoy the view out over the top of the gorge. Eventually you arrive at the track, noted earlier, where you turn left to stroll on to the parking area.

Walk 1b

Crossbill

Practicals

Type of walk: A wonderfully dramatic walk. Short and quite magical. Strong shoes needed after rain. Children and dogs should be under tight control.

Total distance: ¾ mile/1.4km
Time: 1 hour
Maps: OS Explorer 441/Landranger 16

2a

Falls of Shin, Forest and Riverside walk

Park at the Falls of Shin Visitor Centre, grid ref 575994. To access this leave the A837, after Shin Bridge, and follow the B864 to the centre.

The **Shin Falls** have been incorporated into a hydro-power scheme. Fortunately this has been done in a sensitive manner and the falls are not adversely affected. In summer and autumn watch the salmon making their way upstream to spawn. The waterfalls lie in a fine wooded section of the Achany Glen. The river drains the extensive basin of Loch Shin and flows on through the delightful well-wooded valley to reach the Kyle of Sutherland.

1 From the car park nearest to the centre, follow the arrowed way to the Shin Falls, leaving by the main entrance. Cross the narrow road and turn left to descend a slope and then steps to an ornate viewing platform from where you can look down on the dramatic falls below. Return up more steps and turn left to walk along a railed way high above the River Shin to come to another viewing platform, equally well protected. From here you have perhaps an even better view of the falls. Then continue up the slope to join the road a little further along from where you accessed the falls.

Falls of Shin

2 Cross, and continue ahead, over the large extension of the car park, to a gap in the left corner. This gives access into the forest of pine, spruce and beech. Turn left and follow the pleasing path, at first marked with posts with red and green bands, and then, almost immediately, signed with green banded posts. The way climbs gently then descends a little before climbing again to a viewpoint from where you can look down on the River Shin, hurrying on down through magnificent woodland. Go on ascending the easy-to-walk path as it comes beside a little stream, which you cross before bearing round right.

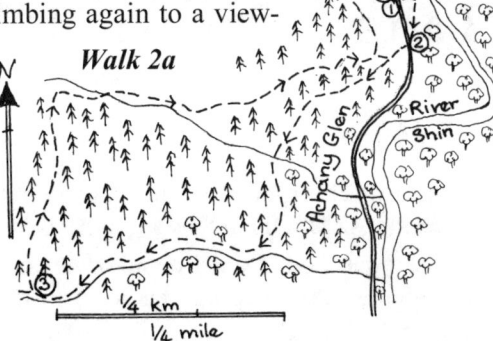

Walk 2a

3 Carry on along the distinct, now generally level track, as it winds a little, before it begins to descend, soon to reach the car park. Turn left and walk with the children's playground to your right. A few steps along take a left turn marked with a blue-banded post. This takes you into superb deciduous woodland and leads you on, gradually descending, to a little gate to the narrow B-road. Cross with care to go through a similar gate and follow the path as it bears steadily right along the side of lovely River Shin once more. Then a railed path brings you back to the road and the car park.

Bullfinch

Practicals

Type of walk: A not-to-be-missed walk. The paths are excellent and the woodland delightful all year.

Total distance: 2 miles/3.4km
Time: 1–2 hours
Maps: OS Explorer 441/Landranger 21

13

2b

The Ord Hill Archaeological Trail, Lairg

Park at the Ferrycroft Countryside Centre, Lairg, grid ref 579063. Access this from the A839.

For thousands of years people dwelt on **Ord Hill** and traces of how and where they lived can be seen on this delightful archaeological trail.

1 Look for the waymaker post, no. 1 at the back of the Countryside Centre and go through a gate to take the grassy path through the rough moorland pasture. As you go look for a small mound on the right, almost covered in heather, and another larger one a short way along on the left (no. 2 marker post). These are probably the remains of Bronze Age round houses. They would have had a turf and heather roof supported by a wall of stone and turf. There would have been many of these houses scattered over the hill. As you walk the trail look for more mounds and imagine the scene, of inhabitants bustling about and smoke rising from their fires and passing through the pointed tops of the thatched roofs of their round houses.

Chambered Cairn, Ord Hill

14

2. Join the main track and begin to climb the hill and when the track divides take the left turn. At no. 3 post look on the left for a burnt mound, a communal cooking place. This would have had a stone-lined pit where water was heated. Stones were heated in the fire and then thrown into the water to cook meat or fish. Carry on climbing gently and follow the path as it winds on around the hill gradually climbing towards the top. As you go enjoy the view across the surrounding fine countryside and then look down to spot ancient banks forming field boundaries.

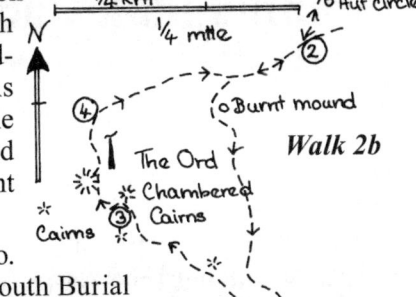

Walk 2b

3. Carry on to the top of the hill (no. 4 post) to reach the site of Ord South Burial Cairn, the cairn constructed 5,000 years ago. All that remains are a few standing stones, once part of the central chamber. Pause here to enjoy the superb view of Loch Shin, Little Loch Shin and the village of Lairg. Wind on along the distinct path and, almost in the shadow of the telecommunications mast, look for a large mound of stones. Look closer and you will spot several long flat stones; these are some of the roof slabs of the entrance passage to the central chamber within the cairn. It was built some 5,000 years ago as well. Here certain members of the tribe or clan would have been buried.

4. Continue on the path, which soon descends quite steeply as a track to pass no. 3 post again. Go on down the main track. As the way flattens out, don't miss the left turn that takes you on past post no. 2. Carry on to reach the Countryside Centre.

Stonechat

Practicals

Type of walk: A pleasing hill climb with much to stir your imagination.

Total distance: 1 mile/1.8km
Time: 1 hour
Maps: OS Explorer 441/Landranger 16

15

3

Spinningdale and Loch Migdale

Park up the little road which runs north-west from the A949 in Spinningdale. There are two places to park, one above the other, about 1 mile/1.5km up the road and on the right, grid reference 665908.

The **Woodland Trust** is Britain's leading conservation charity dedicated to the protection of our native woods. Here they own a substantial area of ancient oak, pine and birch woodland with some moorland and a forest bog, formed from a silted-up loch. The Trust continues to develop trails through the woods.

The old mill at **Spinningdale** is located 8¾ miles/14km west of Dornoch. The village was constructed in the 1790s by George Dempster, of Skibo, to house people working in his cotton mill. He had built the mill to counter unemployment, which was having such a terrible effect in the area. Sadly, because of the remoteness of the area and the high cost of transportation, the venture did not thrive. In 1806 the mill was destroyed by fire. If you wish to see the ruin, continue along the main road for 220yds/200m, east from the village, and look down left. You cannot get down to it.

Spinningdale Mill

Walk 3

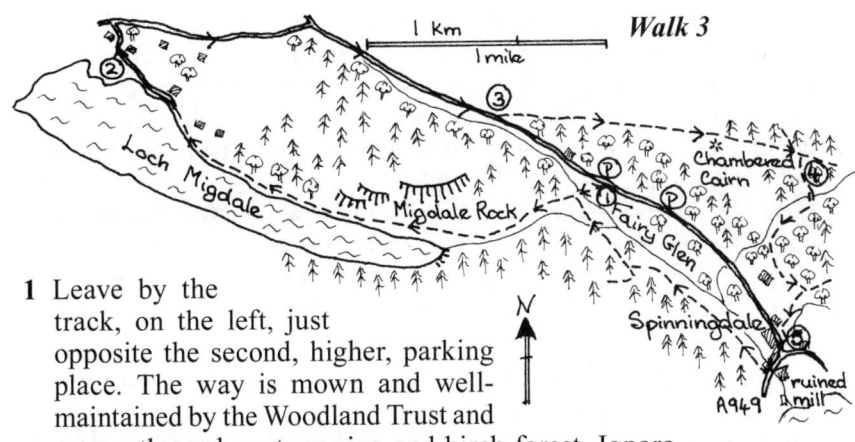

1. Leave by the track, on the left, just opposite the second, higher, parking place. The way is mown and well-maintained by the Woodland Trust and passes through mature pine and birch forest. Ignore two tracks that go off left. Soon Loch Migdale appears on the left through the trees; if you have time walk down to the shore and sit quietly. Here you might spot a kingfisher. Then continue along the delightful way, with the slopes on your right becoming steadily steeper and more craggy, but still with pines on the lower slopes. After about 1 mile/1.5km there is a notice board, marking the end of the property belonging to the Woodland Trust. Continue on the path, with fields to the right beyond a fringe of trees, then join the road running along the very edge of the loch. Look for tufted ducks and dabchicks.

2. Follow the road as it turns away from the loch and go right at the next junction, signed to Spinningdale. Walk uphill through birch woodland, and past occasional cottages, until the road levels off on heather moorland with scattered trees. Bear right again at the next road junction and walk on for about a mile, gently downhill, into birchwood. Go by a small Woodland Trust sign in a passing place then carry on until you can take a waymarked grassy track left.

3. Ascend the delightful way through open pine and birch woodland. Eventually it levels and comes out into more open country with views down to the left and fine views of Creag a'Bhealaich behind. Go past a chambered cairn on the right, which has mostly fallen in but still has a few big slabs showing. From here there is a distant view over the Dornoch Firth. Continue on the track, with scattered pinewood on the left.

4. When you reach a rough track coming in on the left, continue for a few steps to take a waymarked path, on the right. Carry on this lovely way winding down through birch trees. Cross a burn on a newly constructed

bridge and then wind round above the valley with glimpses across, right, to the Migdale Rock. Stride on down to the lower edge of the wood, where the path winds left and undulates a little before reaching a burn crossing with a waymark; there is a tempting gate into a field but ignore this and carry on up the slope on a much rougher path. Follow this until it swings left uphill, just beyond another waymark. Here take an indistinct path, on the right, running downhill between gorse bushes. Go through a gate gap and on down with a burn, below, to your left. Walk in front of a ruin to join a track and follow this across the burn and down to the road in Spinningdale.

5 Walk left to the main road, where you turn right to continue along the pavement. Cross the bridge over the river and walk on past a cottage. Here take a track, on the right, which leads you back into Woodland Trust property. The way climbs through planted pine, then birchwood. Finally it descends to cross the burn on a sturdy wooden bridge. It then runs along a causeway with boggy ground among the scattered pines. At a T-junction, after 1¼ miles/2km from where this track started, turn right on your outward path and return uphill to your car.

Kingfisher

Practicals

Type of walk: Good paths and tracks. There are about 2 miles of quiet road walking.

Total distance: 8 miles/13km

Time: 4 hours

Maps: OS Explorer 438 and 441/Landranger 21

Very pleasant, lovely sands + history trail   Aug 2011

4

Dornoch to Embo

Parking is easy in Dornoch. Leave your vehicle near the Cathedral, grid ref 798816.

Dornoch has been a small holiday town ever since the railway arrived. It became a royal burgh in 1628, its status conferred by Charles I. Before or after your walk find time to savour some of its magic by wandering around the environs of the Square. You will be charmed by the small Cathedral and Dornoch's magnificent red sandstone castle, now a hotel. It is also famous for its extensive golf course and its wonderful sands.

The little village of **Embo** has been a settlement since at least the Bronze Age. It was formerly a fishing village as you can see by the fine harbour, now closed, and when you explore the lanes and rows of little cottages that run parallel down to the beach. Today it is a centre for tourism with families attracted to the large caravan site immediately above the long clean sandy beach.

Dornoch was once the seat of the Bishop of Caithness. **Earl's Cross** is believed to mark the boundary between church land and that of land belonging to the Earl of Sutherland. If you were a fugitive from justice and could reach church land you were able to claim sanctuary in the Cathedral.

1. Walk down the road, with the cathedral to your left and the Castle Hotel to your right to reach the Square. Cross with care to walk the road, Church Street, signed Beach, that goes off in the far right corner. Pass the Dornoch Inn and take the first left turn (Golf Road) to walk between the greens of the magnificent golf course. If the course is very busy and

The Earl's Cross

you are anxious about flying golf balls, carry on along Church Street, and follow it, past Golf Road, and on where it winds round, left, below the course. This joins up with Golf Road at the Beach car park.

2   Look for the track going off, left, signposted to the village of Embo. Stroll on through gorse, then marram and lyme grass, on the right, and the golf course stretching away, left. From here you can look down on a vast expanse of sea and ahead, the lovely sandy bay curving round in a splendid arc. Where the track begins to wind inland, bear right on a grassy trod through the lyme and marram grass. Then take a small path heading right (there are several) down to the shore and enjoy continuing on the delightful sands. Beyond, in the distance, are the wooded slopes of Ben Bhraggie with its monument on top. Across the Firth you can see Tarbat Ness and its lighthouse, the highest on the mainland and built by Alan Stevenson.

3   Stroll the glorious sands, pausing to watch the sprays of water that shoot upwards as gannets dive for fish. Look on the skerries where you might see redshanks 'sunbathing'. Look ahead to where the bay curves round to Embo Harbour to see innumerable gulls resting on the water. When you reach a section of the bay that has been sturdily reinforced by large boulders, take a narrow track up to a ramp from the sands. Beyond, wind right with the curve along a sandy track, with red posts to your left and a painted red line along the grass also on the left of the track. Continue along the track until you reach the end of the golf course, where a gate gives access to rough pasture.

4   Follow the little path through the vegetation to come close to the edge of Embo's large caravan site. Cross a small footbridge, and wind right on a reinforced track. Just before it reaches the shore, take a narrow path on the left and then continue along the shallow dunes towards the harbour. When the way ahead looks 'difficult', descend to the beach and continue to the harbour, with its narrow sandy section where boats can be dragged up and a large pier stretching out to the point. There is no access to this section of the harbour. Wind round to the far side of the

20

harbour and look out to the skerries where turnstones and ringed plover congregate. Walk along the paved way above the shore to the main part of the caravan site. Here you can walk either along the sand or go up and take a raised grassy path along the sea side of the site. At the second flight of steps along the way, turn left and pass between two rows of caravans and then climb a slope to the car park and the entrance to the site onto Hall Road on the edge of the dwellings at Embo.

5 At this point of your walk you might wish to visit the village, where you pass through several ginnels on your explorations. It was here people settled after being cleared from the north and west. Then return to the same part of Hall Road and walk on to take the old railway track, now a walkers' and cyclists' track, on the left. This continues between huge fields of barley or oats and then comes to a cross of tracks. Carry on ahead, where gorse and broom grow along the sides, perfuming the air. The track runs above the golf course. Curve round to the left past a house, then watch out for where the track appears to go ahead to a large barn; this is where you wind a little left and then curve right to continue on a pleasant reinforced footpath.

6 A short way along, take a stile on the right into immature Scots pine. Follow the path as it continues left and after a pleasing stroll through the trees you reach the Earls' Cross where you will want to pause. Continue on, following the path as it steadily veers left and at the next choice of paths go left again to a similar stile out of this pleasant diversion. Turn right to continue on the footpath, soon to pass in front of a row of houses. Then the path and the golf course meet. Here keep well tucked in on the right, for a few steps, and then climb a little slope and walk on to join Grange Road. Follow this ahead where it winds right along Argyll Street to come downhill to the Square in the centre of Dornoch. Cross with care and walk on to return to the Cathedral.

Gannet

Practicals

Type of Walk: Very pleasant circular walk. If the tide is right you can walk all the way from Dornoch to Embo on the sands. If the tide is too high for comfort, there are footpaths all the way above the shore.

Total distance: 6½ miles/9.5km
Time: 4 hours
Maps: OS Explorer 441/Landranger 21

5

Dornoch Point

Park as for Walk 4.

Dornoch, an ancient burgh, nestles at the mouth of the Dornoch Firth. It has an enviable climate for such a northerly point. Start this lovely walk from the Cathedral and very quickly begin your ramble through pleasing saltmarsh to the shore near Dornoch Point. The return along golden sands is a children's paradise not only for building sand castles but also hunting for a plethora of shells thrown up by the tide.

The Dornoch Firth receives the waters of the River Oykel, which is joined by the Shin. The estuary continues eastwards to the sea beyond Dornoch Point. The Meikle ferry once crossed the narrows. In 1809 a crowded ferry capsized and nearly 100 people drowned. In 1991 the late queen Mother opened the **Dornoch Firth Bridge**, 982yds/890m long, shortening the A9 from Inverness to Thurso. The bridge forms part of the boundary between Ross and Cromarty, to the south, and Sutherland to the north.

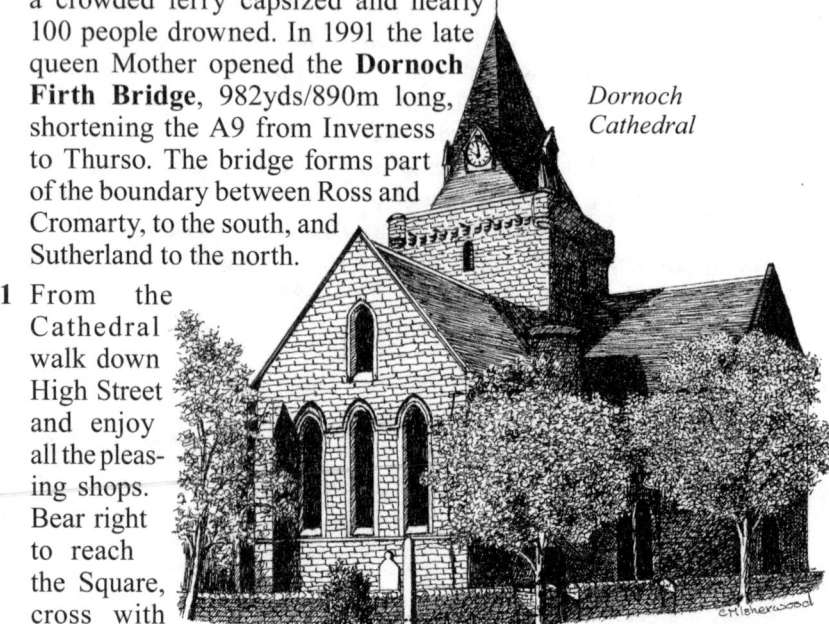

Dornoch Cathedral

1 From the Cathedral walk down High Street and enjoy all the pleasing shops. Bear right to reach the Square, cross with

care to go ahead down Church Street, in the bottom left corner. Walk on to take the third left turn, Carnaig Street, to continue in front of a row of cottages standing on the site of earlier turf-covered cottages. The latter were constructed by the people who had been cleared from their crofts in the north, by their landlord, to make room for a more valuable 'crop': sheep. At the end of the row, wind right to the road and walk right again. Almost immediately, bear left along a narrow road signed to the airport car park. A short way along, take the rough track going off right to join a parallel tarmac road and head on left. As you continue, note for your return, a reinforced track going off left and off right, just before the little airstrip of mown grass.

Curlew

2 Continue on to make a short diversion to view the elegant Dornoch Firth Bridge across the wide firth. Where the road swings left, take a wide grassy track, on the right, which ends at the saltmarsh on the edge of the estuary. From here you have a superb view of the bridge over the Firth, with Struie Hill and The Struie ahead, and of Ben Wyvis peeping over the top. Bird watchers will delight in the variety of waders feeding along the edge of the water or roosting if the tide is high.

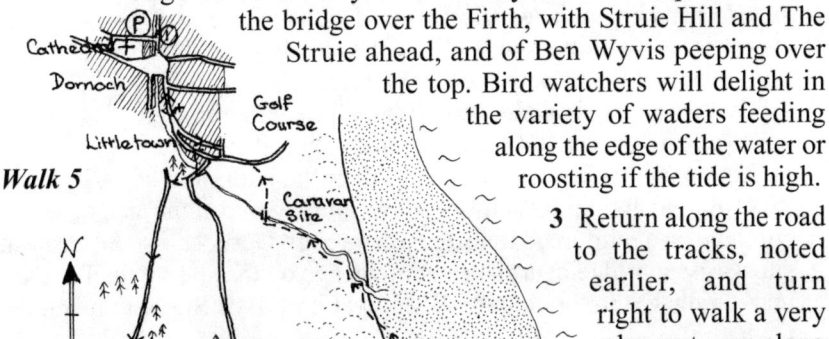

Walk 5

3 Return along the road to the tracks, noted earlier, and turn right to walk a very pleasant way along the edge of the airfield, keeping to the left side of low posts marking the edge of the grassy runway. At the end of the track, pass through the airport car park and in front of a small airport building. Continue beside

more boundary posts that edge a glorious grassy track out onto the extensive salt marsh, with large sand dunes away to the left. Here in high summer look for northern marsh orchid, twayblade, frog orchid, Grass of Parnassus, and ragged robin. At a Y-junction take the right branch, keeping beside the boundary posts and, when these cease, carry on to walk to the left of the last of a row of yellow and white posts.

Grass of Parnassus

4 Follow the grassy trod as it passes small pools of water and where you might spot hoof prints of horse riders using the same path. Along the edge of the path, grows marram grass and more wild flowers. Here you might come across a few clumps of seaweed or perhaps common whelk egg-cases thrown up by the last very high tide or blown in by a gale. Stroll on along the left side of a developing creek and wind a little left and, suddenly, the sandy shore and the estuary come into view, a spectacular sight.

5 Turn left and begin the wonderful stroll along the shore, enjoying all the shells left by the receding tide. Eventually you near the tidal Dornoch River. Just before the river's edge, climb up a little path through the low sand dunes and follow a sandy path through the marram to come beside the river. When the path divides, leave the riverside and climb a low inland sand dune and continue on a reinforced track to pass through Dornoch's small caravan site. Cross a bridge over the river and leave by the site's exit. Turn left and wind right to the Square. Bear right up Castle Street to reach the Cathedral.

Practicals

Type of walk: Very pleasing walk over the saltmarsh, returning along the sandy beach and beside the river. All level walking. If the tide is very high and the sand is under water, return by your outward route. If there is an on shore gale, leave your walk for another day.

Total distance: 4½ miles/7.4km
Time: 2–3 hours
Maps: OS Explorer 438/Landranger 21

6

Balblair Wood

Park in the car park, on the left (east) of the road, opposite the entrance to the wood, grid reference 814977. To reach this drive along Ferry Road south out of Golspie, signed to Littleferry.

Loch Fleet was once a wide open bay, a sea loch that stretched far inland. Currents sweeping south, dragging shingle, gradually reduced the mouth to a narrow channel, through which the tides race. It is noted for its concentrations of sea-ducks in winter. Loch Fleet Nature Reserve covers over 1,000 hectares of estuary and coast. It is owned by the Sutherland Estates and managed by Scottish Natural Heritage and Scottish Wildlife Trust. Together they are restructuring the pinewood at Balblair. This will allow young trees to become established, creating a more varied range of tree ages in the wood.

Loch Fleet

The Mound is a causeway which was built by Thomas Telford in 1816 and has provided a safe crossing of the marshes at the inland end of Loch Fleet since then. Sluice gates let the tide through, and also allow migrating salmon and sea trout to pass upstream.

1. Cross the road and enter the wood by a track between mature pines, with moss, bilberry and heather on the ground. Look carefully at the sides of the track for creeping ladies' tresses, which is abundant in early summer, and for the rare one-flowered wintergreen; 90% of the Scottish population of this flower occur in this wood and it can be seen from the path at the right time of the year. Twinflower, another pine-wood rarity, can also be found here. Cross a bridge over the burn and head on, going straight ahead at a cross of tracks. Look for siskins and spotted flycatchers here. Ignore a track on the left which runs down to the shore. At the next Y-junction take the right branch (the left one is your return route) to continue through younger trees and open areas with views of Mound Rock and Princess Cairn. Cross a less obvious track beside a stand of old pines and walk on. Eventually the track enters a belt of older pines and swings right. Take a small path going left towards the estuary shore which you can see through the trees, following occasional red waymarks.

2. Continue on the path, which runs along the edge of the grass above the shore. Ahead you can see the Mound, and the cliffs and hills around it. Keep on this small path as it winds above the shore for about a mile. At high spring tides some of this may be difficult in places; the best way is across the top of the shingle. The path and the shore swing round from south to east giving a view across the basin of Loch Fleet. Look for shelduck, eiders, and curlews, and if you are lucky, greenshank. In winter you may see long-tailed duck and scoters. Herons are frequent at any time of year, and in summer you may see an osprey fishing.

Walk 6

3 Move into the trees when you reach a fork in the path. If you miss this carry on along the edge of the shore until the shingle turns into pebbles and the going gets quite difficult, and here if you go up the bank you will find a path running along through the trees just above the shore. This winds through the woodland to come out near a cottage, called Balblair. If you miss the path altogether, turn inland across grass when you see the cottage and join the path there. Go past the cottage and along the track to join your outward route. Turn right to return to the edge of the wood and your car.

One-flowered wintergreen

Long-tailed ducks

Practicals

Type of walk: Mostly good tracks and paths. The top of the shore becomes increasingly pebbly as you approach Balblair so walking gets less easy, and at high spring tides it may not be passable; try to find the path through the trees.

Total distance: 4½ miles/7.4km
Time: 2–3 hours
Maps: OS Explorer 441/Landranger 21

7

Ben Bhraggie and the Big Burn

Park in the car park in Fountain Road, Golspie, grid ref 838001. Access this by the A9, which passes through this county town of Sutherland.

Ben Bhraggie is a fine hill and its 100ft/30m statue of the 1st Duke of Sutherland stands on the top of a 76ft/23m plinth. The statue dominates the skyline, particularly Golspie, the village from where this walk starts, and all his lands around. He was not a good landlord, although he did believe he was and that all he did was to improve the land. He drove people off their lands, and burned their houses, to make room for a great sheep run. The people were sent to the coasts and given such small crofts that they had to make their living in other ways.

The **Big Burn Gorge** and its waterfall is Golspie's hidden gem. The dramatic walk through the spectacular gorge is criss-crossed by footpaths. Don't forget to take your camera.

1 Walk on up Fountain Road, past a fine church and a magnificent water fountain, a memorial to the Duchess of Sutherland.

Waterfall, Big Burn

Walk 7

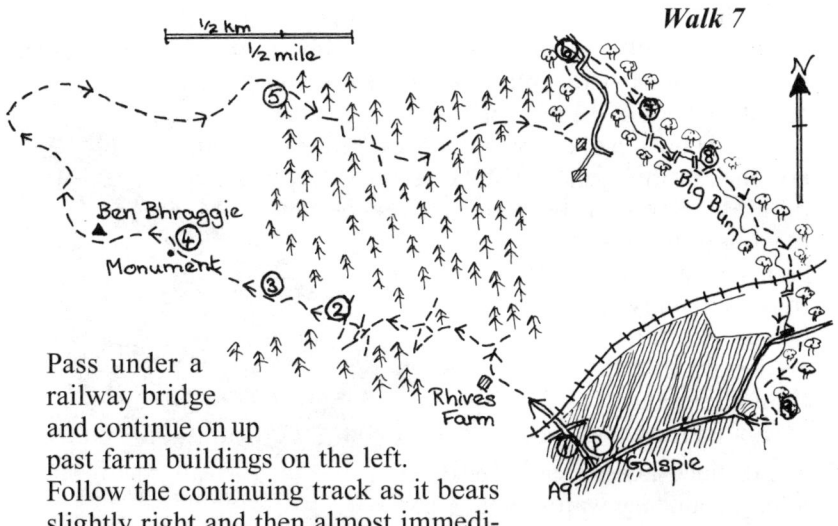

Pass under a railway bridge and continue on up past farm buildings on the left. Follow the continuing track as it bears slightly right and then almost immediately turn left, still climbing to go on, past a huge water tank (reservoir) and on through a tall deer gate. Continue into the forest and where the 'road' makes a large bend, take the signed narrow path, on the right, that leads on up through the trees. Cross a forest road and continue up through the forest. Follow the way as it veers left, close to a power line pylon. Cross the forest road and take the signed path, almost opposite, to cross another almost immediately. Then go on climbing steadily to reach the edge of trees and cross a forest road once more.

2 Go ahead up the steep slope, which has been clear-felled, following a narrow distinct path. It wanders a little left, then right, easing the gradient. Eventually, after stepping up some large boulders, you reach a wooden shelter where you might wish to take your first break, out of the wind and with a splendid view over the forest to the pleasing rolling hills beyond and, also, along the coast and out to sea.

3 Go through the gate beside the shelter and follow the path rising steadily through heather. This last part of the climb, though short, is quite steep but easy underfoot. Then you arrive at the foot of the huge monument on Ben Bhraggie, erected in 1837 to the memory of the 1st Duke of Sutherland. Besides the statue is a very powerful pair of binoculars. Use these to enjoy the view. Focus on the splendid Dunrobin Castle and see if you can count the towers and chimneys. Enjoy the view out to sea and peer up the lower part of the monument and see if you can read the plaque half way up.

4 To continue, stand with your back to the monument and walk a wide

track through the heather. This is level at first and for all its length is a joy to walk. Again the views, this time over extensive heather moorland, are superb. Follow the track as it winds, descending gently, round the back of the hill, making a large curve. Look right to see just the top of the monument over the moorland; as on much of this walk the Duke seems to oversee your progress. Keep on the wide track when you reach a division of paths, the upper one is a trail for cyclists. The lower track descends steadily and keeps beside scattered trees to your right. It then passes through another tall deer gate into pine woodland.

5 The distinct way carries on beside a long boundary wall to your right. Continue on the track as it winds away from the wall and go on to almost reach a narrow road. Here a marker post notes the start of a narrow path going off left, keeping roughly parallel with the road but winding delectably, with many twists and turns, through a belt of well spaced pines. When you can spot the road again the path makes a large curve before descending to join it.

Red grouse in heather

6 Turn left and cross a little bridge over the Big Burn. Bear right and take the lower of two tracks. Follow this hedged way above a house and then into pleasing deciduous woodland. Watch out for an easy-to-miss footpath that turns obliquely right and descends to the side of the burn. Here note the tiny three-armed metal signpost.

7 Turn left and keep beside the burn on your right. This is a glorious path beside the tumbling water and through mixed deciduous woodland with a wonderful mix of flowers in the spring. Carry on the lovely way to reach a bridge across the burn. Pause half way to look down into a huge 'hole' through which the placid burn becomes a raging torrent. Stroll on, beyond the bridge, and go down until you near the next bridge. Before it, look for another tiny three-armed signpost and bear left through the magnificent gorge. A series of rails and fenced footbridges carry you safely on your way to reach the end of a railed platform, which projects out into the burn and from where there is splendid view of the plummeting fall, seen earlier. Return to the bridge and cross. Walk on through the gorge to pass below a long thin waterfall descending in fine trails over green foliage luxuriating in the spray.

8 Press on through the spectacular gorge, crossing sturdy bridges, until the distinct path, now stepped, climbs away from the river and continues on through the pleasing woodland. Pass under a flaring viaduct and on to the side of the A9. Here climb left up the grassy slope to stand on the old bridge, known as the 'Little Bridge', with its monument. The bridge was the rallying point for the Clan Sutherland. Go on over the grass covered bridge to the side of the A9. Cross with care and walk on left up the pavement. A few yards along look for the waymark, set back from the road, to walk a narrow path. Continue on this to climb imperceptibly above the burn, passing beneath gracious beech trees, your boots crunching the mast as you go.

9 At the next waymark, turn oblique right to descend to a stile and on along a track to a road. Bear right to cross the burn and reach the busy A9 once more. Turn left and walk through the long main street and cross at the traffic lights. A few steps left, turn into Fountain Street, on the right, where you have parked.

Primroses

Practicals

Type of walk: A great walk of contrasts – through woodland, up heather slopes, over moorland and beside a wonderful burn.

Total distance: 7½ miles/12km
Time: 3–4 hours
Maps: OS Explorer 441/Landranger 17

8

Dunrobin and Carn Liath Broch

Park in the car park for Carn Liath Broch. This lies on the left of the A9 about 2¼ miles/3.5 km north of Golspie, grid reference 868014.

Dunrobin is a magnificent castle with a definite French look about it. It has 189 rooms. Parts of the castle date from the 1300s. The formal gardens were laid out by Sir Charles Barry, who was the architect for the Victorian extension after he had built the Palace of Westminster. The present owner is Elizabeth Janson, Countess of Sutherland who inherited the castle in 1963 following the death of the 5th Duke.

The **Carn Liath Broch** stands on a terrace overlooking the shore. Its walls, in parts, still stand over 12ft/4m high. It has a well preserved entrance passageway used to guard the broch and the lintels of the doorway are present. It was first excavated in

Dunrobin Castle

the 1800s by the then Duke of Sutherland. At first it was thought to be a burial mound. Then it was decided that it was probably built in the last century BC or the first AD and that it possibly was a defensive structure for extensive families and their livestock.

1 Go through a small gate at the back of the car park, giving access to a crossing over the railway. Cross, with care, and walk up the rough field beside the fence. Go through a gap in a fence at the end, cross a ditch and make your way uphill through newly planted deciduous trees, keeping left of a mature beech tree. In about 55yds/50m, turn right onto a track and after 110yds/100m leave it left. Follow the track uphill to join another obvious one and turn right, with mature pines on the left. Walk for 220yds/200m then wind left up another track leading back through the pines to a memorial erected to James Loch, manager of Dunrobin Estate.

2 Return to the track (the one before you turned left for the memorial) and walk right up into the forest through conifers and some deciduous trees, with broom and gorse lining the way. Look for siskins and coal tits in the trees. At a junction turn left, following waymarks, round a forest gate, and go on downhill. Enjoy the views out towards Tarbat Ness as you go. Keep left at the next junction, wind down through large trees and then into open fields. Ignore a path on the left but when you reach Dunrobin Mains turn left and walk a fine lime avenue to the railway line at Dunrobin Castle Station, the Duke of Sutherland's own private station.

3 Cross the line, then the A9, with care, and head on between the gatehouses and along the drive to the car park in

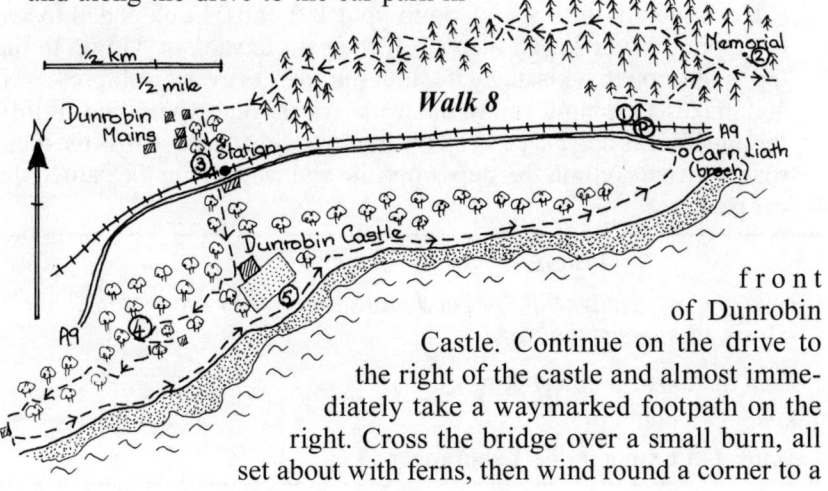

front of Dunrobin Castle. Continue on the drive to the right of the castle and almost immediately take a waymarked footpath on the right. Cross the bridge over a small burn, all set about with ferns, then wind round a corner to a cross of paths, and take the right turn, zigzagging to a higher level. Bear left along the edge of level ground with a steep slope to your left. In early June the woods are a mass of bluebells. Walk on into rhododendrons and then open bluebell wood again, to come down to a track.

4 Cross and follow the small path ahead which runs into young birch woodland. This path winds around (with a detour to the left to a memorial) along the top of the steep slope again. Then take the obvious left turn downhill, using steps to go through the remains of a gate. Walk on beside a garden and out onto a track. The house on the right is called Tower Lodge. Continue through a gate on the left into a pasture and follow the clear grassy way towards the sea. The field is full of buttercups, daisies and speedwell in spring. Stroll on, behind the shore, with the fine trees of the castle grounds to your left, and the castle coming into view. The path runs along behind a low sea wall with the walled gardens of the castle to your left. Go up to the gates and peep in.

5 Carry on along the shore past the old jetty, and go on ahead where the main track turns left. Keep on this smaller path through trees and out into a field which is blue with bluebells at the right time of year, a fantastic sight. Keep ahead along the grassy way into deciduous woodland, ignoring a signed path going left, to reach a gate out of the wood. Follow the way across pastures, where lapwings wheel and call, until the wood to your left ends. Look ahead to see the mound of the broch then stroll the path towards it. Go up to the top, and through a kissing gate, into the site. It is very well preserved and makes a splendid end to the walk. After your explorations return through the kissing gate and up the track straight ahead. Cross the main road with care, climb the steps opposite and walk along the path to the car park.

Bluebells

Practicals

Type of walk: Delightful, on good paths and tracks except for about 110yds/100m near the start.

Total distance: 5 miles/8km.

Time: 2–3 hours

Maps: OS Explorer 441/Landranger 17

9

Morven

Park by the bridge and telephone box at Braemore where there is room for several cars, grid reference 073304. To get there drive along the minor road running west, signed Braemore, from the A9, just south of Dunbeath.

Morven at 2320ft/706m is the highest hill in Caithness, and its unmistakeable conical shape can be seen from many places, including the south side of the Moray Firth. It is an Old Red Sandstone hill, part of a group that contains the smaller but equally fine Maiden Pap and the longer quartzite ridge of Scaraben.

The **Wheelhouse** is just a mound with scattered stones. It would have been an ancient homestead. A more complete wheelhouse, so called because of the arrangement of the stone rafters, can be seen on the walk at Loch Eriboll (Walk 25).

Maiden Pap and Morven

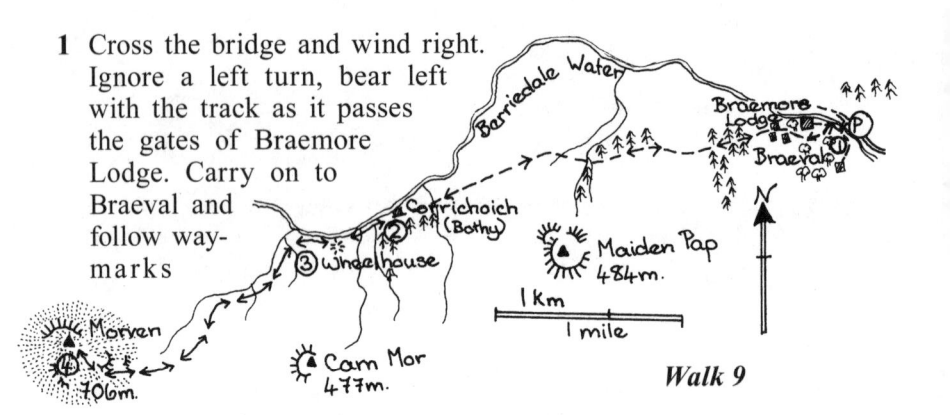

1 Cross the bridge and wind right. Ignore a left turn, bear left with the track as it passes the gates of Braemore Lodge. Carry on to Braeval and follow way-marks

Walk 9

past the kennels and between the keeper's house and other buildings. From August to the end of January you should contact the keeper before going further to check that there is no stalking taking place. Carry on up the track to a gate into a plantation. You are asked to keep dogs on leads as it is a grouse shooting area. Walk through the trees and out onto moorland at the far end. There are oystercatchers, curlews, cuckoos and lots of skylarks. The track is quite easy to walk. It runs below the dramatic peak of Maiden Pap, and soon the equally striking Morven comes into view. Climb gently to the highest point of the track before descending past another plantation to reach the bothy at Corrichoich.

Oystercatchers roosting

2 The track ends here but a vague path continues, crossing various boggy ditches. Head over towards the river and go down to walk across a grassy flood plain. Climb the bank to a grassy mound with stones, which is all that is left of a rather fine ancient wheelhouse. If you feel that the continuing climb to the summit of Morven is too steep and arduous for you, just enjoy exploring the wheelhouse. There is an old homestead of the longhouse type on a nearby mound, and signs of agricultural activity, ridge and furrow, and an enclosure. Then walk back along the track to Braemore.

3 To continue on your climb up Morven, follow the riverbank for another 220yds/200m until a small tributary comes in. Turn left and walk up

beside it, making your way across rough heathery ground, to reach the col below the eastern end of Morven. From here it is a steep rough climb but relatively short. Go up the ridge on heather and then large scree, which is mostly fairly stable. It is probably best to by-pass the knob on the ridge on the south side but it is not difficult to get past; then the ridge up to the summit is easier. The view from the top is extensive and magnificent.

4 Return the same way, with care.

Cuckoo

Cross-leaved Heath

Bell Heather

Practicals

Type of walk: Very easy along the track. The climb up Morven is short but steep and on scree and boulders, and the walk from the wheelhouse to the col is across pathless heather, although not too difficult.

Total distance: 9 miles/14.5km.
Time: 6–7 hours
Maps: OS Explorers 444 and 450/Landranger 17

10a

Dunbeath Village

Park in Dunbeath near to the metal footbridge, grid ref 166293. Access the village by a right turn, off the A9, to pass under the viaduct carrying the A-road. There are toilets at the harbour.

Dunbeath harbour was built about 1800 and by 1815 it had 155 boats anchored there. At one time ice was cut from the river in winter and stored in the **ice-house** ready to preserve the catch of the fishermen. Look for the **statue** of the boy carrying a large salmon over his shoulder. It is a tribute to Neil M Gunn (1891–1973), who was born in Dunbeath and went on to become an influential Scottish fiction writer. His book 'Highland River' tells of the boy Kenn and his lengthy wrestling with his catch, a huge salmon, while searching for the source of the Dunbeath Water. The **Girnal** was a store for grain from the surrounding crofts to be delivered to ports elsewhere.

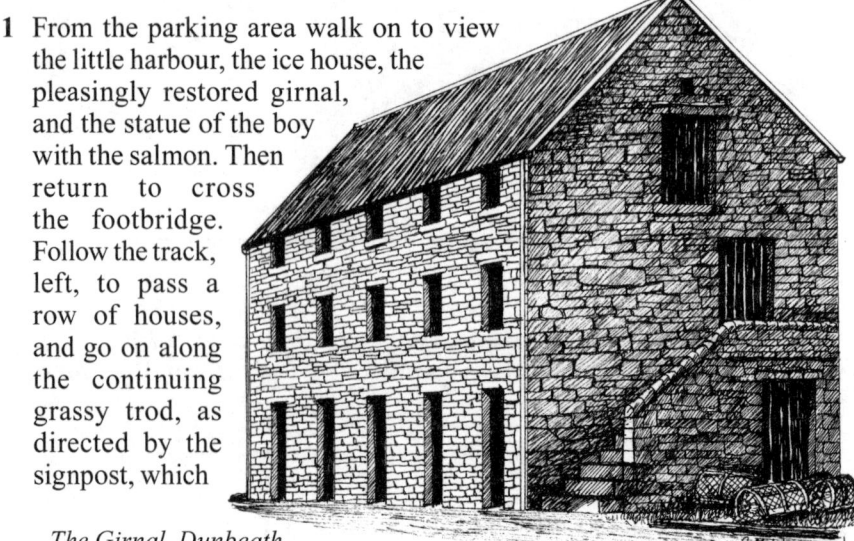

1 From the parking area walk on to view the little harbour, the ice house, the pleasingly restored girnal, and the statue of the boy with the salmon. Then return to cross the footbridge. Follow the track, left, to pass a row of houses, and go on along the continuing grassy trod, as directed by the signpost, which

The Girnal, Dunbeath

directs you to 'The Cave ¼ mile/½ km'. The path is a joy to walk with grass-covered low cliffs to your right and the rocky shore to your left, the path lined with colourful wild flowers in summer.

Walk 10a

2 The path ends at a magnificent Caithness sandstone cliff which projects in front of a sheltered grassy hollow. In the cliff face are several large holes and a small arch through which you can pass to the shore and continue on to a cave before making your return to the green area. The huge cliff looks as if the next storm will break through the holes and the arch and bring down the whole edifice. This is a lovely corner for a break and to watch the wheatears, curlews and fulmars.

Wheatear

3 Return along the shore and before the footbridge climb a narrow path that leads up to a large sign for where a cable comes ashore. Go on climbing the path, wind round with it, and on up to join the old A9 at a sharp S-bend. Walk up the road to the Heritage Centre, attractively housed in the old school building. It is well arranged, very interesting, and the staff are most helpful. After your visit return down the path, cross the footbridge and enjoy the little harbour once more.

Practicals

Type of walk: A very satisfactory short walk with lots of interest.

Total distance: 1½ miles/2.5km

Time: 1–2 hours

Map: OS Explorer 450/Landranger 17 (and a part also on 11)

10b

Dunbeath Archaeological Trail

Park by the Meal Mill, upstream of the Telford Bridge (1812), grid ref 159299. Access is by either of the two road turn-offs in Dunbeath, depending from which direction you approach. Continue until under the A9 fly-over, where there is a turn off and take this for the parking area beyond the old mill.

Prisoner's Leap gorge

The **mill** was built in the 1850s and was worked until 1950. The Cunningham family ran the mill, the last of whom was Adam Cunningham who, in spite of loosing an arm in World War I, returned to work it. The mill lade runs around the back of the field beside the mill. A sluice was built across the river to an island to regulate the supply of water to the mill. At the time of writing the mill is being restored.

In 680 AD the siege of Dunbeath is believed to have taken place by Brude, a Pictish king and it is possible that it was the **Dunbeath broch** that was besieged. This stands high on a little hill between Houstry Burn and Dunbeath Water. The ruin was consolidated in 1990 and a wall was built round it to keep out stock.

The gorge was formed in the last ice-age. It is known as **Prisoner's Leap**. The story goes that Ian Gunn was imprisoned by his enemies, who said they would release him if he jumped the gorge. By doing this he would fail and kill himself, saving them the job. He didn't fail.

1 Take the wide grassy track upstream with the river hidden by bushes to the left. About 150yds/140m along, notice the mill lade, all beautifully constructed of Caithness slabs. Here a sluice was built across the river to an island to regulate the supply of water to the mill.

2 Go on along the path and notice traces of stonework on the small mound to your right, Chapelhill, believed to have been an old monastery, mentioned in Neil Gunn's book, 'The Silver Darlings' (herrings). Continue past a shallow weir and then cross a fine suspension bridge over a craggy drop in the river bed just before the Houstry Burn unites with the Dunbeath Water. Go through the gate immediately on your right, at the end of the bridge, to climb (bracken allowing) to the Dunbeath broch.

3 Return down the hill, go through the gate and descend rock steps beside the river, under the sheer side of the hill, which gives you a good idea of the excellent defensive position of the broch. Carry on through a kissing gate to the strath, where in high summer the bracken lies back from the path but is still occasionally tiresome. The river is now wide and shallow, brown with peat, where you might spot dipper and yellow wagtail. The higher slopes of the strath are lined with steep forest. Closer to the path hazel, birch, rowan and bird

Walk 10b

cherry line the way, a haven for birds, and on either side of the path there is a wealth of colourful flowers, ferns and mosses. Here in a field, in the past, village celebrations took place such as school and church outings.

4 Beyond the next gate is a seat, where you may like to pause, and then the path carries on beside a tall, long wall, beautifully constructed with every cam in place. Ignore the next footbridge and stroll on with a fine view of the hills to your left; in high summer the heather is a wonderful haze of pink. Ahead you can see the start of the dramatic gorge, known as Prisoner's Leap. Just before it starts, the path appears to divide. Take the right branch and begin the long climb, with care, to the pasture on top of the cliffs. The path continues along the edge of the gorge where more care should be taken and ends at a fence. Turn right beside it and walk over the pasture to join a wide track.

5 Walk left, through a gate, and continue on the level way in the direction of two huge pointed cairns that you can soon see on higher ground to the right. After passing a wall on the right, step right over a ditch and head up through the heather, for a short distance, towards a large mound of boulders and the two modern cairns. This is the site of Cairn Liath, a long two chambered burial cairn with a few upright stone slabs still standing. The whitened stones with pink heather all around and the silent moor with dark hills away in the distance, has a wonderful atmosphere of its own.

6 Return to the track and look, right, along it as it begins to wind left towards the eye-catching white cemetery, Tutnaguail, overlooking a beautiful part of the river, which you might wish to visit, but this walk begins its return here. A short way back along the track, after passing a small birch wood to your right and then an isolated birch tree, look for four large stones and a white one, also on the right. Leave the track here and very soon pick up a wide grassy path that keeps left of the single birch and then slants easily down the hillside. Follow it all the way to the riverside. Here just before the river enters the gorge is a flat area with the ruined remains of an old croft, barn and cornkiln. You can also see traces of raised beds, part of the run-rig system of farming. A short distance along, through bracken, you can reach the stony beginning of the gorge and peep into it.

7 Take the same path to regain the track and continue, right, to go through the gate, taken earlier, and continue on for a mile to where it becomes tarmacked. Press on past a farm and follow the road as it winds left and then right to cross the Houstry Burn. Curve right again to pass

another farm, Rhemullen. At the Y-junction keep ahead, right, along another quiet road until just before it winds sharp left. Here, take a hedge-lined track, right, and descend to reach the start of a metalled road and several houses. Wind a little right and then curve left along the road.

8 Where the road turns sharp left in front of the derelict hotel, step right to go down a hedged footpath to the reach the old A9. Curve right at the corner, before the Telford Bridge and take the signed way to the parking area at the Meal Mill.

Dipper

Practicals

Type of walk: A splendid walk that is full of interest, through a lush valley and then up onto moorland. Care should be taken as you climb the cliffs of the gorge and also as you walk above it.

Total distance: 6 miles/9.5km
Time: 3–4 hours
Map: OS Explorer 450/Landranger 11

11

Suisgill and the Strath of Kildonan

Park on the wide verge on the left (west) of the road 220yds/200m beyond the renovated house above the Suisgill burn, grid reference 893252. To access this drive up the A897 from Helmsdale towards Kinbrace. Look for the Baile an Or on the right where you might like

Suisgill Burn

to stop to look at the area where the gold prospectors lived, and then drive on a further 3 miles/5km to the parking area.

Gold rush in Kildonan. In 1869 a gold prospector called Robert Gilchrist came home to Helmsdale from Australia and discovered gold in the Kildonan Burn. This caused great excitement and over 300 men seeking to make their fortunes set up home in wooden shacks at Baile an Or – the Town of Gold. Not a great deal of gold was ever discovered and no one made a fortune, although people still go panning there today and sometimes find a few grains. Most of the digging took place along the Kildonan Burn, just south of Suisgill.

1 Walk back down the road past the house and go left beyond it, across the grass before the river. Head towards the river bank and follow a clear grassy track, with a sheep pen to your left. About 220yds/200m up the burn, cross a wide bridge, not shown on the OS map. Walk along the pleasant wide grassy track above the burn, which runs through birch, rowan and aspen. Skylarks sing and meadow pipits perform their parachute display.

2 After a mile the Suisgill Burn swings right with a tributary continuing straight ahead. In this area there are said to be some of the remains of the old gold workings, which you may like to investigate, although you are unlikely to find much. Cross the burn, on stones if the water is low but otherwise you may have to paddle. The track goes on faintly up the far bank but you take a small path following the burn to the right and on up into the moorland. It is faint in places and sometimes quite eroded, especially where it crosses steep slopes, but it does run all the way up the valley. If you are worried about it, climb out of the valley and walk through the heather at the top of the bank. The river is delightful with small falls and pools and many trees.

3 After a while the river valley widens beyond a small fall. Cross the flat land, and go over the burn, which begins to meander over the flat

valley bottom. When you get tired of crossing and re-crossing the burn, look up to your right to see the line of a track running across the hillside above you, and make your way uphill to join it. Turn right and walk the track uphill, then down to a col and up again, after which the sandy track descends gently along the hillside. There is a wide expanse of heather moorland, quite bleak in some conditions, but you are likely to see many red deer, red grouse and maybe mountain hares. The view up the Strath of Kildonan opens out and distant mountains can be seen. Behind is Morven. There is a small reservoir to the right, then the track crosses a bridge and descends more steeply above birch woodland, finally zigzagging down through beech and Scots pine to reach the road by a small electricity building. Turn right and walk up the road.

4 At first the river runs closely beside the road, but after 220yds/200m they separate. Here, drop down the grassy bank, left, to walk along beside the river, which is lovely, fast flowing with rapids. Sand martins and swallows skim the surface, common sandpipers and oystercatchers call and you may see a greenshank. Mergansers fly over and teal swim in the shallows. The path crosses ditches on small bridges. Go through a small gate beside a deer fence and continue along the bank. At the end of the deer fence pass through three field gates together by a sheep pen and then turn right to walk up by the Suisgill Burn towards the road. Beyond a gate, turn left to return to your car.

Mountain Hare

Practicals

Type of walk: A pleasant walk, mostly on good tracks. The path by the second part of the Suisgill Burn is very small and eroded in places, and after that you have to find your own way across the moorland for a short distance. Stalking takes place on the Suisgill Estate from August 1st to February 15th and you are asked to contact the estate office on 01431 831217 to enquire about access.

Total distance: 6 miles/9.8km
Time: 3–4 hours
Maps: OS Explorer 444/Landranger 17

Forsinard Flows, the Dubh Lochan Trail

Park in the small car park at the visitor centre in the Station Building at Forsinard, grid reference 891425. To reach this drive along the A897 which runs from Helmsdale to Melvich on the north coast.

The Dubh Lochans and the Ben Griams, Forsinard

The **Flows** are the vast wild peatlands of north Scotland. Peat is made up of dead plant material, which has not decayed because of the cool and permanently saturated conditions. The cool moist climate of this part of Scotland is ideal for its growth. Peats were cut here (and still are) and taken via the railway to distilleries all over Scotland where it was used to malt the barley for whisky.

Dubh lochans are the small pools, often quite deep, which occur in frequent groups in these peatlands, forming a mosaic of land and water and providing a unique habitat for wildlife. They may be named black (dubh), but on a sunny day they are sky blue and in late spring they are bright with bogbean.

Walk 12

Bog bean

1. Have a look round the **visitor centre**, in the old railway station building, where a warden will tell you about the reserve. Then go across the level crossing on the very quiet road, and 110yds/100m on turn right following a sign for the Dubh Lochans Trail. This is now paved throughout with Caithness Flagstones and so is very good underfoot, although the flags can sometimes be slippery. The path wanders across the wet moorland, crossing peat cuttings and then climbing slightly. Away in the distance the peaks of Ben Griam Mor and Ben Griam Beg dominate the view.

2. Walk left at a junction as directed by a small arrow. You are now in the middle of a maze of small pools,

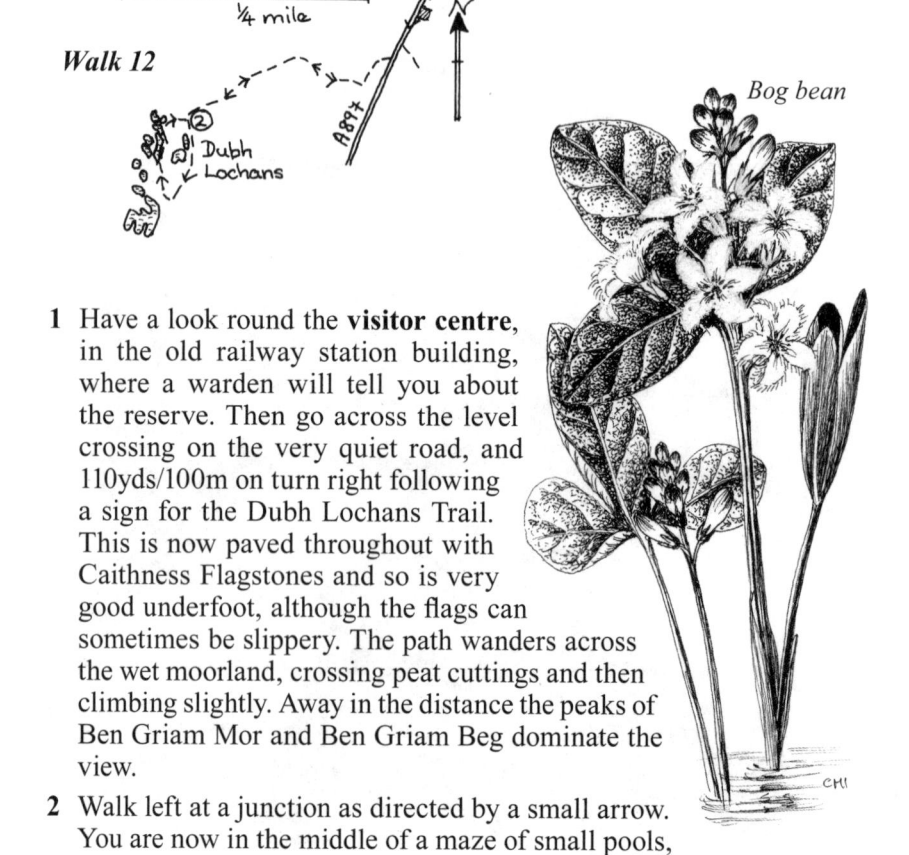

the dubh lochans. Look for dragon and damsel flies. Skylarks sing, and you may hear the mournful peep of a golden plover. The path winds around between the pools, coming to a dramatic wooden seat and then back to join the outward path. Turn left and retrace your steps to the road and your car.

Hen harrier

Practicals

Type of walk: The trail is very good underfoot and flat. It is very interesting and well worth doing for an easy glimpse into this wild remote area.

Total distance: 1 mile/1.5km
Time: ½ hour
Maps: OS Explorer 449/Landranger 10

13

Rumster Forest

Park in the forest car park, grid ref 206397. Access this by the A99, leaving it north on a minor road just west of Lybster, signed to the A9 and Sheppardstown.

Rumster forest was originally planted with pine and spruce in the late 1940s, on ex-crofting ground. These trees soon filled into a solid mass. Today much of the forest has been cleared and replanted with birch, rowan and scots pine, opening up views to the North Sea coast. During the replanting many archaeological remains were exposed.

Rumster Mill

1 Turn left out of the car park and walk down the road for ¼ mile/0.5km to take an easy-to-walk track into more of the forest. Heather, and very green moss, line the track, but don't step off as it is very wet on both sides. As you go look for pine marten droppings. After an open area you enter a compartment of tall, dark, closely planted sitka spruce. At the end of these trees take the immediate right turn.

Walk 13

2 Carry on the track to go by derelict but picturesque Rumster Mill. Just beyond is a large grassy mound, the remains of a broch. From here you can see the sea beyond a loch. At the next T-junction, turn right and continue. After ½ mile turn left. Here to the left is a little mound and behind a few trees stands a picnic table from where you can look down on vast acres of immature Scots pine. While they are so young you have a fine view of the valley below through which passes a sparkling burn, with pastures on either side. Head on to pass derelict Golsary farmstead, on the left. Just beyond, step into the undergrowth and walk ahead, with some difficulty, for a few steps to cross a sturdy footbridge over the burn to visit a well preserved grass-covered broch. After a little exploration return over the bridge to the track and carry on bearing steadily right.

3 Climb gently to pass a small quarry of bright red sandstone, attractively colourful against the young self-seeded spruce. Continue up past a striking cliff face on the left, where there is a seat beside the track. Then you reach another derelict farmhouse with a drying kiln behind. Close by is a clearing with a picnic table. Wind up the track and look

Treecreeper

51

back down to this pretty corner. Press on, steadily upwards towards the very obvious TV beacon. In the few deciduous trees here you might spot bullfinch, coal tit and spotted flycatcher.

4 Go on over the brow, ignore the tarmacked track to the beacon and walk right on the tarmacked road descending to a T-junction, where you bear left and stroll on to the road, which you cross to reach the parking area.

Coal tit

Practicals

Type of walk: A pleasing walk, on good tracks. Ideal for a day when you need shelter from a tiresome wind.

Total distance: 4 miles/6.5km

Time: 2–3 hours

Maps: OS Explorer 450/Landranger 11

14

Munsary

Park close to Loch Stemster, grid ref 186421. To access this take an east turn off the A9, south of Achavanich, and look for the parking area on the left about half a mile ahead.

The information panel at the start of the walk says that in the past the crofters lowered the level of **Loch Stemster** so that they could remove the mud and nutrients from the bed. This was added to their acid soils to provide better grass to feed their animals.

Munsary Cottage was built around 1860 for the Duke of Portland as a hunting lodge for his grouse shooting friends, providing shelter from the wind and the rain, and somewhere to eat their picnics. Today it acts as a scientific base for research on the flow country; the group owning it hope that one day they will be able to restore the building and equip it suitably.

Achavanich Standing Stones

1. From the little parking area walk on along the track with the loch to your right. Go past a small jetty and a boat, hauled up on the bank, and then look across the loch to see, on the other side, an old

Walk 14

Red deer stag

crofthouse, Achkinloch. Notice the fields around it, a green oasis in the tawny bleached moorland. Carry on by a small lochan where bogbean thrives, and follow the track over a low brow. A ditch runs along either side, supporting a variety of plants and sphagnum. Where the vegetation has been swept away by the water you can see, under the turf, and at the base of the ditch, thin plates of Caithness flagstones. As you continue use the small information boards that pull out from the sturdy waymarkers.

2 As the easy-to walk track descends steadily you can see, over a wide expanse of flow country, Ballachly farm and then further away the white painted Munsary Cottage, the aim of the walk. Eventually the track winds right, just before a pretty lochan, where yellow irises thrive. Go on steadily descending to pass more fine green fields where the moorland seems to be pushed back and drystone walls have been built to stop its further incursion. Look to the far left, just before the farm to see a walled cemetery, a strange sight in such a lonely place. To the right is a mound, the remains of a broch. Stride on past the farm with its bright red doors.

3 Descend steadily and follow the winding path as it drops gently through the moorland. Watch out for red deer and notice their footprints along wet patches in the track. Go past a small mound of peat; this is still cut and used for heating. And then a short rise brings you to Munsary Cottage. The building is enclosed by a stone wall and there is a stone bench outside

providing some shelter and comfort for walkers who have made it to the end of the track. Sit on the bench and look ahead to the foot of the hills, rising up from the moorland, to see the remains of several old crofts, from where people were 'cleared'. Go over to the wall to the left of cottage and peer, left, to see Munsary Dubh Lochs, small pools that sparkle in the sunlight.

4 Then begin your return, back along the track, enjoying the wide skies, and large open views across the moorland, to the parking area. Before you leave, walk or drive 200yds/180m, south-east, along the road to a magnificent stone circle, believed to be 4,000 years old. It is unique in that all the stones stand sideways on to the centre. A little above the circle and approached by a stile is a chambered cairn, believed to be a 1,000 years older than the circle. This is a magical site and rounds off an excellent day's walking. There is a small parking area opposite to a passing place and several excellent information boards.

Short-eared owl

Practicals

Type of walk: An unusual walk, on a good track. The route is waymarked but there is no possibility of getting lost. As you go ponder on the lives of the people who lived in the ruined crofthouses that you can see over the moorland – perhaps the reason for the large cemetery seen before you reached the farm.

Total distance: 6 miles/9.5km
Time: 3–4 hours
Maps: OS Explorer 450/Landrangers 11 and 12

15

The South Yarrows Archaeology Trail

Park in the car park at South Yarrows Farm, grid reference 306434. The trail is signed from the A99, Latheron to Wick road. Turn west as indicated, then left, and at a T-junction left again past Loch Brickigoe. The farm and car park are at the road end.

There are various **archaeological artefacts** to be seen, such as a broch, several hut circles, three circular chambered cairns, a standing stone, the site of a hill fort and two long chambered cairns. Caithness, being flat and relatively fertile, was well populated in ancient times, from the Neolithic through to the Iron Age. There is much evidence of the people who lived here scattered around the countryside and in some places such as here at the Hill of Warehouse, there are concentrations of remains.

The Broch, Loch of Yarrows

1 Go through the gate in the corner of the car park and downhill to another gate. Follow the waymarks down the next field to a gate in the bottom left corner which gives access to a broch. This is an unusual broch with various buildings round the edge and an outer wall. It is partly flooded because the level of the loch has been raised artificially. You may see curlews and lapwings.

2 Go back through the gate and walk along the bottom of the field to a bridge over a ditch, full of irises and meadowsweet and kingcups. Pass through a gate gap. Beyond, follow the waymark and look for a low circular bank marking the base of an old roundhouse. Cross the fence by a stile and follow the path as it winds up over a knoll, then another. Climb another stile and go downhill to a third. As you walk uphill from this stile look on the left to see the remains of a roundhouse and buildings, all rather overgrown.

Walk 15

3 Carry on uphill; it is quite steep and boggy. Cross another stile and continue. Near the top of the hill take a small path on the left, marked with an arrow, to go round to a chambered cairn. It is very steep; there is a low mostly blocked entrance and you can peep over the sides where they are grassy to see the hollow in the middle. Go on to the next one 55ft/50m away. This one is less intact. It is marked with a neat modern cairn.

4 Head on down the path to another stile. Look left to see a standing stone with another lying beside it and, to the right, stands a third chambered cairn. Cross a boggy area, full of bog asphodel, and climb up along the side of a hill where, above, there are scant remains of a fort in the heather. Carry on the path below low cliffs, then along a lovely ridge with a fine view, north, over lochs to the Caithness coast.

5 Gradually descend to a ridge with a long cairn on it; this is an amazing heap of stones with many, mostly collapsed chambers. Then continue along the path to another, which is just a long irregular grassy mound

but has the entrance structure, of Caithness flagstones, showing at one end. From here the path turns sharply right and goes downhill to a gate onto the road by the car park.

Lapwing

> **Practicals**
>
> *Type of walk: A fascinating glimpse into the land use and lives of people up to 5,000 years ago. The trail is mown and in places there are flagstone slabs over the bogs, although it can still be quite wet. The views from the top are excellent.*
>
> *Total distance:* 2 miles/3.4km
>
> *Time:* 2 hours. There is so much to see. Allow plenty of time.
>
> *Maps:* OS Explorer 450/Landranger 12
>
> **NB** Please respect the farmer's privacy and work by not taking photographs or drawing pictures of him, his family or his buildings, leaving gates and fences as you found them, and taking care not to disturb animals. Please do not bring dogs.

16

Noss Head and Girnigoe Castle

Park close to the little harbour at Staxigoe, grid ref 384525. Access this by heading north across the bridge over the Wick River in the centre of Wick. Then take the first right turn, which is signed for Broad Haven, Papigoe, Staxigoe and Noss. At each following T-junction take the signpost for Noss until the final turn left which you ignore to drive on into Staxigoe. Go past The Pole and the village hall and park on the hard standing.

Staxigoe was once the largest herring station in Europe and created work for many craftsmen, but when bigger boats were built, these looked for better harbourage along the coast at Wick. The Pole on the harbour edge was constructed as a **barometer** and was used by fishermen to determine the conditions at sea. The houses of the village were built of sturdy Caithness flagstone and the **unique red roofs** were created from tiles brought in on Dutch boats as ballast and replaced by outgoing cargo. The houses around the harbour were demolished in the late 1940s and most of the families were rehoused in council-built modern houses.

Castle Sinclair Girnigoe

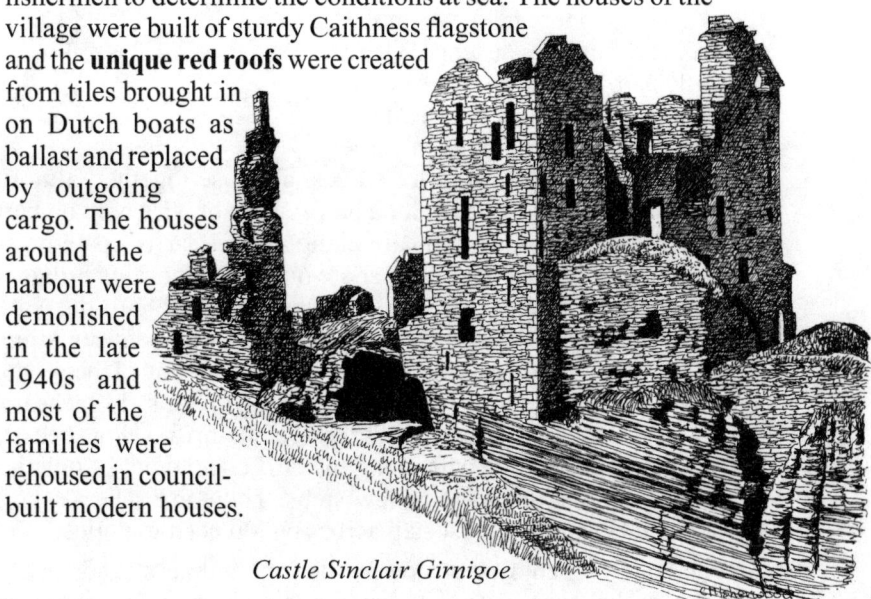

59

The **lighthouse**, built in 1849 and engineered by Alan Stevenson, has ever since guided shipping past the treacherous waters around Noss Head.

Castle Sinclair Girnigoe, visited on this walk, was first known as Castle Girnigoe. It was built for William Sinclair, the 2nd Earl of Caithness in the latter half of the 15th century, before his death at Flodden in 1513. In 1606 an Act of Parliament was passed to change its name to Castle Sinclair. It is a magnificent ruin which at present is being restored.

1. Walk north along the edge of the little harbour and continue where a notice welcomes walkers. Follow the good track to pass right of the farmhouse and then wind on through outbuildings. Pass through a gate to walk a faint path along the cliff edge. Look down on the several bays you pass to see the innumerable grey seals cavorting in the water or basking on the rocks far below. Pass through the next gate. Ignore an old stile and remain inside the wire fence.

2. Carry on into a large field, where the crop comes almost to the fence. There is a little path beside the latter but it needs care as there is a dry shallow ditch in places. Just before you come to the wall ahead and two wire fences, all close together, almost at the end of the huge field, look for a half section of wire with no barbs. Climb this and continue with care along a short narrow path outside the wire, with a drop to the rocky shore on your right. This brings you to some wire netting which you step over with ease into the Nature Reserve. Here the cliff edge is fenced but there are no fences running across the rough pasture. What there is, at the right time of the year, is a wonderland of colour. Look for marsh and frog orchids, dwarf heather, devil's bit scabious, hay rattle, bird's foot trefoil, thrift, yellow bedstraw and tormentil. There is a path along the cliff edge, though sometimes you have to move inland for a few steps. There are several ancient shallow ditches that you just step across but do need to notice.

3. As you continue, enjoy the superb cliffs of Caithness sandstone and note the stacks, cone-shaped and crowned with grass. When you spot

the lighthouse at Noss Head, which is surrounded by a long wall, head for an obvious gate in the wall by slanting, left, away from the cliff edge. Beyond the gate, walk towards the lighthouse on a track that soon emerges from the grass. Pass through two more gates, walk on a few steps to turn right to view the lighthouse, which is privately owned.

4 Then turn round and follow the access track to go through a large gate. Walk on along the reinforced way to reach a small car park, on the left, and go right along a track to the remains of dramatic Castle Sinclair Girnigoe. The ruins are magnificent, the sandstone walls glowing rosily in the sunlight. After viewing all that is visible, return along the track and turn right to walk the long narrow road, virtually traffic-free, through large flat fields on either side. The boundaries of these are constructed of interlaced large flagstones of the local rock. Go past Noss farm, on the right, almost hidden by sheltering sycamores. Carry on the long straight road for 1½ miles/2.3km from the castle access track and follow the road as it winds left and continues for another ½ mile/1km to reach the war memorial at Staxigoe. Turn left at the cross roads just beyond, to return to the attractive little harbour where you have parked.

Frog orchid

Practicals

Type of walk: Delightful along the cliffs but the path can be rough in places. Choose a day when the wind is blowing off the sea rather than the land. Wear suitable clothes, for the wind off the North Sea can be cold. Walking boots or strong shoes essential to walk the rough pasture along the cliffs and in the nature reserve.

Total distance: 5 miles/8km
Time: 3–4 hours
Maps: OS Explorer 450/Landranger 12

17

Stacks of Duncansby

Park in the large car park in the centre of the small village of John o' Groats, grid ref 380732. Access this by the A99.

The village of **John o' Groats** is often believed to be the most northerly tip on the British mainland, whereas in fact Dunnet Head is further north. The name of the scattered village is believed to have been derived from Jan de Groot, a Dutchman who was in charge of the ferry to Orkney in the 15th century. On a sunny day the white painted souvenir shops, cafes and other buildings contrast pleasingly with the blue sea of the Pentland Firth.

Duncansby Head, a wonderful grassy headland of very high flagstone cliffs, provides innumerable nesting sites for hundreds of birds. A delightful grassy swathe takes you round the fenced cliff edges towards the superb off-shore sea stacks, named Tom Thumb, Muckle, and Peedie.

1 From the car park, walk down to the shore and continue, right, along a path that might be rough and quite difficult after high tides and on-shore wild storms. If parts of the path have been completely washed out, you may have to start the walk after passing

The Stacks of Duncansby

Walk 17

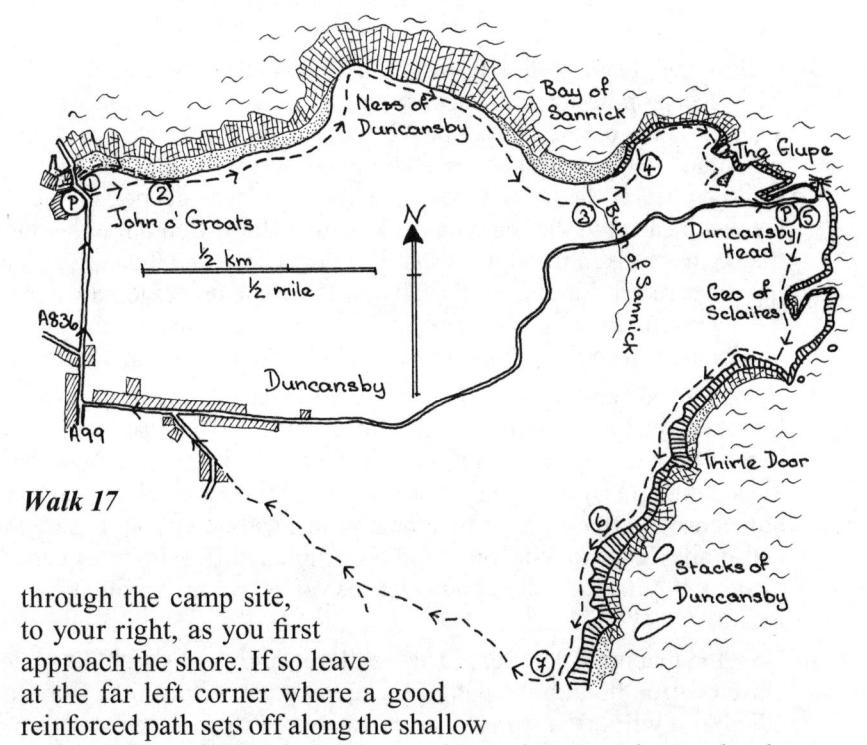

through the camp site, to your right, as you first approach the shore. If so leave at the far left corner where a good reinforced path sets off along the shallow cliffs of a raised beach. Shortly you descend steps and meet the shore path climbing gently and then the two proceed as one. Very soon you have excellent views of the island of Stroma and an extensive view of Orkney. Go through a gate and on to cross a stream by steps and a flat bridge.

2 The excellent grassy trod continues to Ness of Duncansby Head, a low promontory jutting out into the Pentland Firth. Pause on the seat, watch the grey seals and read the interesting information panel. Carry on the lovely way, from where you might spot both arctic and common skuas, and on the shore, redshanks, oystercatchers and eiders. As you near the Bay of Sannick notice the beautiful shell sand beach, golden against the red rocks. The path keeps above the bay and becomes rougher where small streams find their way down to the shore.

3 Here, if wishing to sunbathe or picnic, and to continue the walk, take a narrow sandy path leading down the side of a wide gully, through which flows the Burn of Sannick, easily stepped over, to reach the beach. Otherwise, keep on just above the beach to pick up an easy path slanting steadily up the side of the cliff, at the far end of the bay, to climb a stile over the fence.

4 Follow the grassy path, left, inside the fence and wind round the cliff edge. Keep on beside the fence, cutting off a corner of one large green sward to come beside The Glupe. This narrow, very deep ravine, stretching inland, supports much vegetation and nesting ledges for fulmars. Wind on beside the fence to look into the next, even deeper, ravine. At the end, nearest to the sea, you can see the natural arch through which the sea has broken through, at first forming a cave and then undermining the roof until it eventually falls in. Continue on diagonally across the sward to reach the road and turn left for a few steps to the nearby Duncansby Head lighthouse, constructed by Alan Stevenson in 1924.

5 Cross the road and walk onto the turf as directed by a signpost. Climb a little to reach the trig point (198ft/64m) and then go on, inside the fence to pass another dramatic sea inlet, the Geo of Sclaites. Head on down the sloping grassy swathe with fine views of the spectacular Stacks of Duncansby. After a pause here begin the steady climb up beside the continuing fence to wind on round even higher cliffs with more superb views, enjoying the colourful flowers as you go before passing through a gate.

6 Now the fencing is left behind and children and dogs should be under close control, though the path does keep you a fair distance from the edge. You will often want to pause to look at the pointed stacks and marvel at the force of the sea and the winds that have shaped them. The moorland stretches inland to your right and in August is ablaze with sweet-smelling heather, interspersed with devil's bit scabious. When you are parallel with the last stack, Tom Thumb, its top like an ancient castle, and where the path comes close to the cliff edge, look for a narrow path leading into the moorland.

Fulmar

7 It goes straight ahead through the heather, with a few damp patches to cross. After 220yds/200m you need to step up a peat bank, athwart the path, to the start of the peat road, indefinite at first. It soon becomes a distinct embanked raised track, with peat cuttings to either side and where colonization with plants is taking place. When a stream joins the track the way becomes wetter but eventually the water slides across the track and moves away into the moorland. Soon you can see some of the scattered houses of the village. Here the track becomes really wet, so tread warily until you reach a grassy area and then the road at its end. Walk on down the metalled road to

join almost the start of the road to the lighthouse. Turn left, walk past the sports field and continue to the A99, where you turn right to carry on for half a mile to the car park in the centre of the village.

Sneezewort and Devil's-bit Scabious

Practicals

Type of walk: Magnificent. A glorious walk on long grassy swathes. The path over the moor, though wet in places, makes it into a fine circular walk. Remember that the weather can change quickly and the winds change direction so dress appropriately – warm clothing and strong shoes.

Total distance: 5 miles/8km
Time: 3–4 hours
Maps: OS Explorer 451/Landranger 12

18a

St John's Point and Scotland's Haven

Park on the right on the wide grassy verge where the narrow road turns sharp left to a small teashop, grid ref 312744. There is room for 3 or 4 vehicles. Access this from the A836 by a narrow road west of Gills Bay and just east of East Mey.

The **Pentland Firth** is 12 miles/19km long and 6–8 miles/9.5–13km wide. Here tidal waves race at varying speeds from 6–12 miles/9.5–19km an hour. When the eastern and western currents meet the waves sometimes rise into the air, a magnificent sight. Off St. John's Point is a line of skerries called the Men of Mey, which contribute significantly to the turbulence.

Stroma lies 2 miles/3.3km from the mainland. In 1862 a remarkable tide climbed the 200ft/61m cliffs and swept across the island. You can see houses on the island but now they are all deserted.

Tower o' Men o' Mey

Scotland's Haven is a natural harbour, which is cut off from the sea at low tide.

1 Go through the gate in the corner of the grassy layby and walk ahead for a few steps. Take the grassy path, left, heading

66

for the sea. Follow the pleasing smooth swathe with heather on both sides. Go through a gate and continue along the path as it winds across pasture. Very soon you reach a dilapidated wall along the foot of a mound, which is believed to be the site of an iron-age fort. Just before the path runs round to the right side of the mound, look down to a small bay below and then follow a grassy path down to the beach, where you will want to linger. Here there is a small man-made harbour, an old winch for landing the herring and up under the cliff face, the remains of the medieval chapel of St John.

2 Return up the grassy path and wind on, right, below the mound. The path is narrow and care should be taken. Continue on over the pasture to keep right of a deep narrow geo and on to St John's Point to enjoy its dramatic view. Look left to see Dunnet Head. Orkney lies ahead and John o' Groats and Duncansby Head, right. Close at hand is the depopulated island of Stroma. Sit on the rocks at the tip of the Point and look down on the flagstone skerries that stretch out menacingly into the sea which swirls angrily round them. These rocks, known as the Men of Mey, continue out into the Pentland Firth. This is where the waters of the firth collide and cause tumultuous seas.

3 Return over the pasture to go through the gate taken earlier and walk ahead for six or seven steps. Turn left on a very narrow path through gorse and heather. The way is wet in parts as it winds steadily right. Eventually it leaves the scattered gorse behind and moves out on to drier heather moorland, still heading right, and with a fence away to the left. Beyond is the sea and another wonderful view of the islands and the coastline. Keep on along the narrow but distinct path and follow it as it still keeps to the right of the fence and begins to wind round Scotland's Haven. Pause here to look down on the sea inlet and its sandy bay, where seals bask and prepare for giving birth in November.

4 When the high level path comes almost to the top of the cliffs, with the sandy bay to your left, look for a similar path heading sharp right, through the heather. The start is indistinct but almost immediately becomes easy to follow as it climbs over Mey Hill. Eventually the roofs of the teashop and other

Walk 18a

67

buildings come into view. Almost at the gate to where you have parked, the path disappears in little pools. Pick the driest way to regain the parking area.

Grey seal

Practicals

Type of walk: Superb, particularly in August when the heather covers the moor and its perfume fills the air.

Total distance: 2 miles/3.4km

Time: 1–2 hours

Maps: OS Explorer 451/Landranger 12

NB Two miles west stands the Castle of Mey. This was bought by the Queen Mother in 1952. She renovated both the castle and its garden. In 1996 she handed the castle, its 200 acre estate and her herd of Aberdeen Angus cattle to a charitable trust. It is well worth a visit, but do check that it is open to visitors. The food in the café is splendid.

18b

Castlehill Flagstone Trail and Castleton Community Trail

Park at the small Castlehill Beach car park, grid ref 195686. Access this by the A836 and then take a narrow turn, north-west, at grid ref 201682.

James Trail started the Flagstone Industry at Castlehill early in the 19th century. He lived at fine Castlehill House, which was destroyed by fire in1967. The stone was obtained from the quarry, which ran from below the car park by the wood and extended up through Castletown for nearly a mile.

The **harbour** was built in the 1820s to ship flagstone. At first it was sent to ports down the east coast of Scotland and England but as it became famous it was exported all over the world. The Strand and the concourse of Euston Station were paved with Caithness stone, which was famed for its durability.

Caithness sandstone, which splits into thin slices or flags, occurred about 370 million years ago. A great lake covered the whole of the north of Scotland and out into the North Sea. Successive layers of sediment were formed. Between the layers the lake dried out leaving the subsequent planes along which

Old Windmill, Castlehill

69

the rock splits. The Castlehill workers raised the flags by hand held levers. Some of the flags used to build the harbour were quarried at low tide.

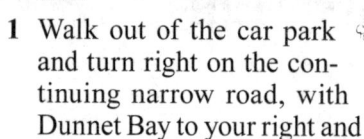

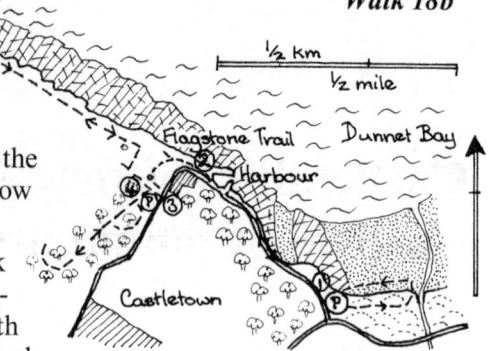

Walk 18b

1. Walk out of the car park and turn right on the continuing narrow road, with Dunnet Bay to your right and a high stone wall to your left. This very soon brings you to the little harbour, where you will want to pause. Carry on to the corner of the road and look towards large derelict Castlehill House where, at the time of writing, restoration is taking place. Some parts of the building have been completely restored and now house the Heritage Museum, which is open 3 days a week from 2–4pm (Tel 01463 702250).

2. At the corner do not turn, but go ahead on a track that leads into the derelict site of the old Castlehill flagstone works. Follow the path round left and climb to a seat on a viewing platform with a good view of Dunnet Bay. Return to the path and walk on to pass, on the left, the site of the waterwheel and sluices deep in rampant vegetation. Carry on up a gentle slope to see, the old dam that fed the waterwheel and then continue to the base of the old windmill, beautifully reconstructed but without the wooden cabin that supported the sails and turned them to catch the wind; the waterwheel, the dam and the windmill were all used to provide energy for the works. Continue to the road.

3. Walk right and immediately go right again to walk down a track lined with Caithness flags. Bear right with the track to pass the end of a row of cottages where some of the workers lived. Go on to wind left to walk just above the shore of the bay. You may wish to follow this easy-to-walk walled way with wonderful views over the sea and of Dunnet Head. If the tide is receding you are likely to see ringed plovers, knott, green plovers and curlews. Overhead fly both skuas, shags and gannets. This track runs for nearly a mile to reach an old 1939–45 war outlook building now a ruin. Return by the same track to the side of the road.

4. Turn right and right again into an enormous car park. Head towards the far left corner to take a narrow path that passes through part of the old quarry, almost completely colonised by vegetation. This is the start of

Castletown Community and Sculpture Trail. There are some sculptures among the great variety of trees of this delightful woodland; in 1996 twelve hundred hardy native species were planted. Look for buckthorn, willow, birch, rowan, ash, sycamore, beech, alder and whitebeam. Take the path ahead, gently climbing, to pass below the lovely trees. Go right at the top and wind round right to a seat to look out over the bay. To return, wind left and, very soon, left again to return to the start, or you may wish to explore several side turns, ignored on the way up. At the large car park, turn left, wind round the corner to return to where you have parked.

Great Northern divers

Practicals

Type of walk: Short and very interesting.

Total distance: 4 miles/6.5km
Time: 2–3 hours
Maps: OS Explorer 451/Landranger 12

19

Strathy Point

Park in the car park provided at the end of the public road before the lighthouse, grid reference 827686. To reach this turn north on a minor road from the village of Strathy, which lies on the A836 about 10 miles/16km east of Bettyhill and 4 miles/6.5km west of Melvich. The minor road runs along the narrow point towards the lighthouse at its tip.

The **Scottish primrose** is a tiny, beautiful plant restricted to the north coast between Cape Wrath in Sutherland and Dunbeath in Caithness, and Orkney. It is only found within 1 mile/1.05km of the coast, probably because sites further inland have been cultivated. It grows in short grassland which is grazed by rabbits or sheep; it cannot compete with taller plants. Its flowers are deep purple-pink and can be found in late spring and early summer.

Stathy Point

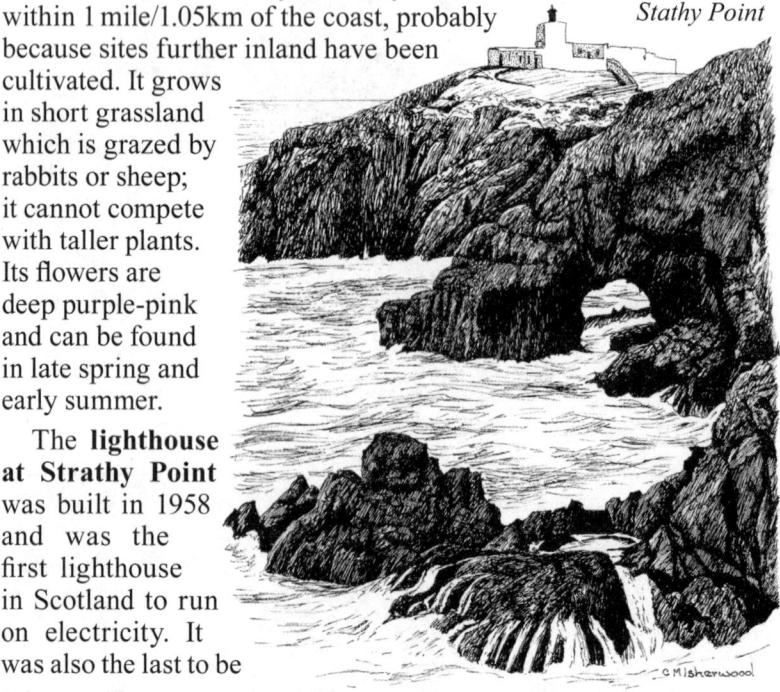

The **lighthouse at Strathy Point** was built in 1958 and was the first lighthouse in Scotland to run on electricity. It was also the last to be built as a manned lighthouse. It is now privately owned and the light is remotely controlled from Edinburgh.

1. Walk on along the road, which is private from this point, although walkers are welcome. You are, however, asked not to take dogs. Go past a cottage and on through fenced fields. Beyond a cattle grid the fence comes to an end. A few yards further on take a clear sheep trod on the right leading across the short grass towards the cliffs. Look back for a fine view of cliffs and stacks towards Strathy Beach and climb the low ridge which runs along this side of the narrow peninsula. There is a shallow lochan between you and the lighthouse. Go to the right of a wartime concrete building and down a gentle grassy slope towards the point. If you want to go right out you will have to scramble along a narrow rocky arete, which is airy but not difficult, to gain a wide grassy promontory. The cliffs are spectacular, and in spring and summer you may see many seabirds, such as gannets, auks and fulmars. Shags fly past and eiders bob in the waves. The maritime grassland has masses of the Scottish primrose and the lovely blue spring squill in May, June and July.

Scottish Primrose

2. Return up the valley below the lighthouse to the road, cross and go to the left of a garage, to climb a low hill. From the far side of this there is an excellent view of a large natural arch, with the sea pounding through. Continue down into a hollow and up the far side, then walk on west along the edge of the fine cliffs. There are animal tracks which make the walking easier although on the short turf it is all quite easy. Look back at intervals; if the tide is right you may see a spouting cave shooting its plume of spray into the air long after the wave has begun to recede. You have to walk inland at intervals to go round deep-cut geos, often with caves at the top. You may see rock doves flying in and out. There is a narrow neck of land leading to another promontory, which you could visit

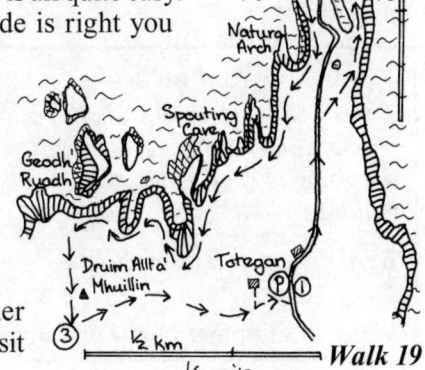

Walk 19

with care if you wished, then climb up and down to a boggy area. Cross and walk up the far side by a fence which has suddenly appeared; there is plenty of room between it and the cliff edge. The next geo has another natural arch, a narrow one this time, and then there is a large steep sided L-shaped island just cut away from the coast. Soon after this the fence turns left. Follow it uphill to the top of Druim Allt a'Mhuilinn, where there is a trig point on the far side of the fence. The views are splendid in clear weather, to Ben Loyal, Ben Hope, and mountains beyond.

Rock Dove

3 Continue beside the fence down the far side of the hill. It turns left; follow it down to a gate. Walk half right here towards another fenced enclosure but keep well to the right of this fence to avoid the boggiest ground. Join a vague path which leads to a farm track. Follow this to the road where you turn left to the car park.

Spring squill

Practicals

Type of walk: A short walk but allow plenty of time to enjoy the scenery and wildlife. It is mostly pathless, or on small paths, but the going is easy. Care must be taken on the cliffs, especially with children. No dogs.

Total distance: 3 miles/5 km.

Time: 2 hours

Maps: OS Explorer 449/Landranger 10

Bettyhill and Creag Ruadh

Park in the car park off the road to the pier, grid reference 705624. To access this, turn off the A836 in Bettyhill to go past the police station and a shop. Just beyond a pool, turn right on a track and 110yds/100m further on is the car park.

The low cliffs and calcareous sand-blown grassland round Bettyhill are well-known by botanists for the fine variety of **flowers** which grow there. Many of these are montane species which here on the north coast grow in profusion at sea-level. Late spring and early summer are the best times to visit and enjoy the wonderful profusion.

From the mid-1700s until 1992 there was a **sweep net fishery** operating in the mouth of the River Naver, catching salmon as they came up river. North from the pier are the remains of an ice-house for storing the fish, a dwelling and a store.

The Ice House, Invernaver

1. Return to the road and turn right. Walk down to the road above the shore, where the old pier stands below you to the left, and there is a fine view across the River Naver to the lovely beach and dunes on the far side. Look over the bank in front of you, in spring and summer, to see the splendid display of flowers on the lime-rich soil. There are scabious and hay rattle, clover and self-heal, and, most exciting, the uncommon purple oxytropis with its silver-green leaves and large red-purple flowers. Turn right and follow the track to look at the ice house and netting station. These are unsafe and you should not go in.

   Walk 20

2. Return 11yds/10m and take the path, now on the left, which runs on along the hillside, through flower-rich machair, with orchids and grass of Parnassus. Here rabbits keep the grass short. Take the right fork at the junction, although the paths join again later. Arrive at a geo with high cliffs to the right and a low point to the left, which you can walk out along. Then return to the head of the geo and climb up a slanting path beside the fence; at the top turn left and walk along above the cliffs, with a wall to your right. Where it joins the fence pass through a gate and carry on along the path. There are several paths but the one that is nearest to the cliffs gives the best view. Look for oystercatchers and curlews, and maybe an otter. Out on the sea you may see scoter, velvet scoter, and long-tailed duck, especially in late summer or spring. Gannets fly past and dive.

Purple oxytropis

Velvet scoters

3 Walk on to the narrow point at the end of the headland and enjoy the view on both sides. To the left there is a natural arch on Neave Island, and, to the right, fine stacks on the next headland. Then return across the narrow neck of land and climb easily up the short grass above the spectacular cliff, where fulmars nest. Look in the grass for the diminutive Scottish primrose, with tiny rosettes of leaves and deep purple flowers. Climb to the summit of the hill. Ahead there is a fence, so make your way over the grass towards it, then drop down into a valley beside it and go round the end of it above the cliff. Climb up steeply again, wind left and pick up a path, which follows the cliff edge. This gradually descends, until you can see another fence ahead with a stile. Make your way down to it; it is rather dilapidated at the time of writing so either step over the fence or go down a bit further and climb a wooden section of fence at the cliff edge. Walk up a distinct path from either point, to a picnic area, and return up the track from here to the car park.

Creag Ruadh cliffs

Practicals

Type of walk: In spite of it being a short walk allow plenty of time to savour it all the way; it is a gem.

Total distance: 2 miles/3.4km
Time: 2 hours
Maps: OS Explorer 448/Landranger 10

21

Rosal Clearance Township and the King's Stone

Park in the car park provided by the Forestry Commission at grid reference 691427. To reach this drive along the B873 to the junction with the B871 at Syre. Cross the bridge over the River Naver and turn right onto a forest track. The car park is about a mile along this track.

The name of Strathnaver is linked with some of the notorious mass clearances, which took place all over the Highlands some 200 years ago, generally to free the land for large-scale sheep rearing. At this time approximately 340 families with a total population of more than 2000 people lived in the Strath, the vast majority in small villages, the land being worked communally.

Rosal township and Ben Klibreck

Rosal township was a thriving village which housed 15 families. It was cleared by the Sutherland estates between 1814 and 1818. Today the site is found in a large clearing in the middle of a forest plantation. There are 47 buildings on the site and information about them is given on plaques.

1. Walk south out of the car park and cross a cattle grid into the forest. Turn left immediately onto a path which zigzags uphill, then winds through the Scots pine trees and contours along the hillside. You may find droppings with rowan berries which could be pine marten. In about a mile the path merges with another from the right and reaches the large clearing where Rosal township once stood.

2. Go through a small gate into the grassy clearing, which has never been planted so is relatively easy to walk. The path winds uphill to the left through the old ruins, with information boards at intervals. You can go wherever you like but it is worth following the trail, partly for the information boards which are very interesting and also for the duckboards over the boggy areas. Look for piles of stones cleared from the fields, and the house ruins with low walls round the kailyards, or vegetable gardens. At the very top of the trail is a chambered cairn, now grassed over, evidence of very long usage of this area. There are fine views to Ben Klibreck and over Strath Naver to Ben Loyal from the top of the clearing. You might like to have your picnic up here, with skylarks singing and a buzzard soaring overhead.

3. On the way down a board tells about peat cutting and there is a section of duckboarding leading into the bog ahead, to a place where peats have been cut. Take care to return from here to the information board to regain the trail which does not continue through the bog. At the bottom of the hill is a corn-drying kiln.

After exploring the township leave through the same gate and follow the path which branches left from the one you came on. It leads out to a forest track. For a short walk turn right here and make your way back to the car park.

4 However, if you want a longer walk turn left and follow the track along above the River Naver. Look for an ancient hut circle. After about 2 miles/3.4km the track winds slightly left and here on the right is the King's Stone, Clach an Righ. It is part of an old stone circle, but most of the stones have fallen and are flat on the ground. Only the King's Stone and one other remain standing.

5 Return to the car park by the outward track, missing out the village on the way.

Skylark

Practicals

Type of walk: Easy on good paths and tracks. The part through the old township is quite rough and can be wet, so wear stout shoes.

Total distance: 2 miles/3.4km to the township and back. 6 miles/9.5km if both parts are done.

Time: 1½ hours and 3 hours

Maps: OS Explorer 448/Landranger 10 and 16

22

Ben Klibreck

Park in a layby 650 yds/600m north of Vagastie (a single lonely dwelling), on the A836, Lairg to Tongue road, grid reference 537288. There is room for 3 cars. Please do not block the passing place. If this is full there is also room for a few cars opposite Vagastie. There is also a car park some distance north by a plantation.

Ben Klibreck (3151ft/962m) is a huge, isolated, sprawling mass of a mountain, dominating the lonely uplands of central Sutherland. It forms a long ridge stretching from Loch Naver in the north to Loch Coire in the south, with a steep rather featureless slope to the west and cut into corries on the east. Its highest summit is Meall nan Con.

Meall nan Con, Ben Klibreck

1   Cross the road and go over the River Vagastie on the footbridge. Walk up beside a tributary of the river on a rough and often wet path. There is a narrow gorge to your left with two lovely waterfalls. Higher up cross the burn on convenient stones and follow the path, on the other bank, through an open gate in a fence. The burn becomes deep and canal-like and it, and the path, wind away to the left towards a loch.

Walk 22

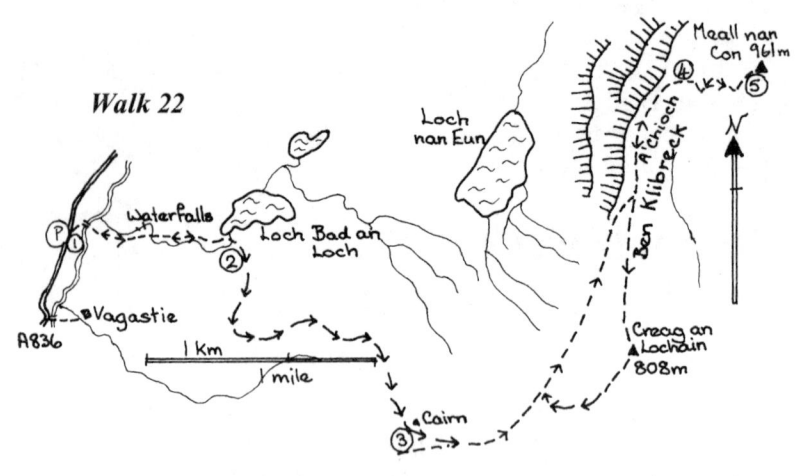

Just below the outflow of the loch there is a wide stony area in the burn and you should cross again here.

2 Keep with the path as it goes on ahead, but soon leave it and bear right for a low rise in the ground, the beginning of a spur, using such faint paths as you can find. Climb the spur and head left along the top over rough heathery and boggy ground. Continue on the top, winding right, soon to join a small but distinct path running along the broad crest and up to a col. Keep on the path to wind left through peat hags and climb to a cairn. On the way up look for dwarf birch, alpine bearberry and cloudberry.

3 From the cairn, head for a path going up the next rise through peat hags easily passed. Climb the steep path and follow it as it begins to swing left, levels off, and then becomes a delightful high-level contouring path. Walk along it with care, enjoying the fantastic views, to reach a col. Head on the path as it rises up the next crest, called A'Chioch, walking over pleasing moss and short grass. Look for mossy cyphel.

4 Scramble over a rocky step and then continue on an easy path to cross a short stretch of boulder field on the final 660ft/200m pull-up to the summit. As you go look for ptarmigan and listen for their motor-bike-like calls. There are crags on either side of the summit and a short ridge. Off to one side is a small bothy, which is useful for shelter on a windy day. The views are stupendous.

5 When you have finished enjoying this superb panorama return to the col below A'Chioch. You can either go back along the contouring path, or if you still have some energy, walk ahead up the next summit, Creag an Lochain. This is very easy over mossy heath. There is nothing to mark the top, but turn right and walk down the gentle slopes to reach

a flatter area. Carry on right, heading for the way you came up and ignoring a path which runs straight ahead to the south down an obvious spur. When the ground gets steeper, head slightly right and suddenly just below you is the contouring path used on the ascent. Turn left along it and retrace your steps to the car.

Ptarmigan in summer

Practicals

Type of walk: A very pleasant mountain, once you have crossed the wet lower slopes. However bear in mind that this is a Munro and fairly isolated.

Total distance: 8 miles/13km. Stalking takes place from mid-August to mid-September; the number to call for information is 01549 411251.

Time: 7–8 hours

Maps: OS Explorer 443/Landranger 16

23

Ben Loyal

Park carefully in the large space before the cattle grid, 110yds/100m down the road to Ribigill Farm. Do not block the gate. To access this take the old road from Tongue which goes round the head of the Kyle of Tongue. About 1.5 miles/2 km south of Tongue, take the private road on the left which goes to Ribigill Farm and drive along it until you come to the cattle grid, grid reference 584547.

Ben Loyal is a magnificent mountain with an unmistakeable craggy outline. It is not particularly high, only just reaching Corbett height, but its isolated position and dramatic appearance more than compensate for this. It is the only igneous mountain in this area, composed of a form of granite called syenite. This has weathered into tors typical of granite country and causes the spectacular shape of the mountain.

Lochan Hakel at the head of the Kyle of Tongue and overshadowed by Ben Loyal, is supposed to contain over £13,000 in gold coin, thrown there by the French crew of a ship, the *Hazard*, bringing the gold from Louis XV of France, as payment for the Jacobite troops who had been

Ben Loyal

unpaid for months. The *Hazard* was chased into the Kyle of Tongue by a Royal Navy Frigate. The ship was destroyed by cannon and the survivors captured by the local Mackays, loyal to the English king, but in spite of much searching the gold, possibly in the deep waters of the loch, has never been found. Three weeks later the Jacobites were defeated at Culloden.

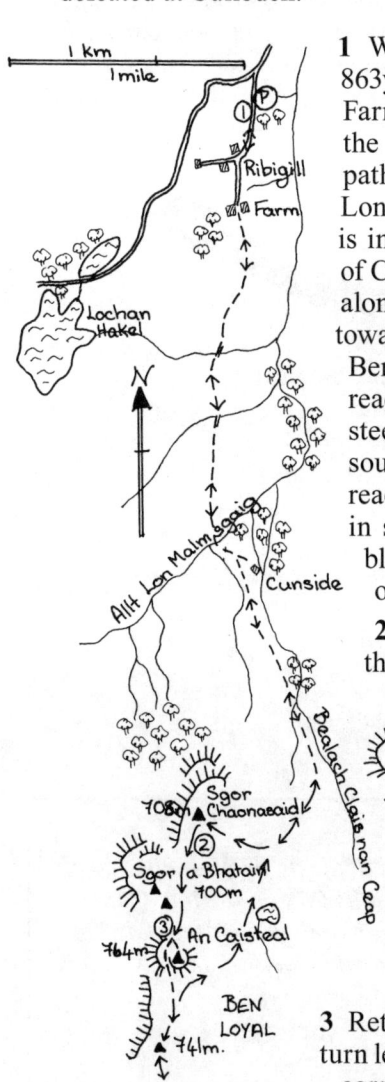

1 Walk on down the road and after 863yds/800m take the left fork to Ribigill Farm. Go on past the farmyard and follow the rough track leading south. It becomes a path crossing the moorland. Cross the Allt Lon Malmsgaig (which may be difficult if it is in spate), with the old shepherd's cottage of Cunside off to the left. Carry on by a burn along a narrow path, which climbs steadily towards the Bealach Clais nan Ceap, between Ben Hiel and Sgor Chaonasaid. Before you reach the bealach turn west and climb very steeply up grass and heather to the col just south of Sgor Chaonasaid. Bear right to reach its rocky summit. Look for ring ouzels in spring and summer and listen for their blackbird-like calls. There are fine views over the Kyle of Tongue.

2 Return to the col and continue along the airy ridge towards the two tors of Sgor a'Bhatain. These are also encircled by cliffs but can easily be by-passed on the east side. The next summit, An Caisteal, is the highest point on Ben Loyal. Walk towards the west side of the craggy tor and scramble up a small path winding left through the granite rocks to the summit. The views from here are magnificent.

3 Retrace your steps down from this point and turn left to contour below the summit above the corrie on the west side. Continue along the narrow but easy grassy ridge to the next top,

85

Beinn Bheag, which is rounded and straightforward. Ignore the ridge running west from here which leads to Sgor a'Chleirich, a spectacular tor surrounded by cliffs but not an easy route. Instead go on to the final peak along the main ridge, Carn an Tionail.

4 Return along the ridge to Beinn Bheag. From the col between this and An Caisteal descend to the right, diagonally down the steep slopes, by-passing An Caisteal, to walk above a lochan and then reach a level area below Sgor Chaonasaid. Look for the four-petalled dwarf cornel in late spring. Carry on down your outward route to the Bealach Clais nan Ceap and on down to Cunside and Ribigill.

Ring ouzel

Practicals

Type of walk: This is a steep but not particularly difficult climb with an exhilarating ridge walk over the various tors on the top. Care must be taken as with all hill walks in this remote country. The burn Allt Lon Malmsgaig may be difficult to ford in wet weather. No dogs should be taken on this walk.

Total distance: 9 miles/14.5km

Time: 7–8 hours

Maps: OS Explorers 447 and 448/Landranger 10

24

Ben Hope

Park in the car park, grid reference 462477, on the small road that runs from Hope in the north, to Altnaharra in the south. Do not be put off by the grass in the middle of the road or the fact that the passing places are not surfaced. The car park is 110yds/100m south of a large barn on the east side of the road.

Ben Hope (3039ft/927m) is the most northerly Munro and is a splendid mountain, with its summit surrounded by cliffs, except on the southern side, where a relatively easy slope leads up to the top. On the west the cliffs drop in two huge rocky tiers almost to sea level, and on the east they are sculpted into fine corries.

Dun Dornaigil Broch is one of the best preserved brochs in Sutherland with its walls standing in places over 20ft/6m high. It has a narrow doorway with a huge triangular lintel stone but you cannot go in; the entry is blocked. It is beside the road about ¼ mile/0.5 km south of Alltnacaillich where the alternative path from Ben Hope comes down.

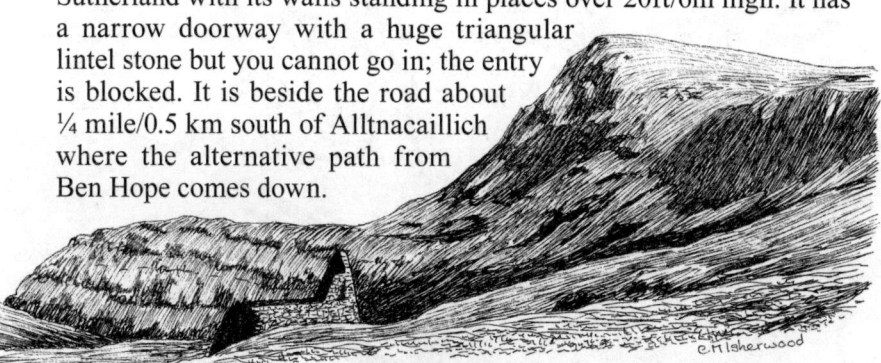

Ben Hope and Dun Dornaigil

1 From the back of the car park, take the path that leaves between two large boulders, signed 'Way up Ben Hope', and continues across the grass beside a burn. Follow the path as it climbs beside spectacular waterfalls to the left. The way is distinct but steep and rocky, like a staircase in places, although there are often little paths to the side round

the steeper bits. Be prepared for some mild scrambling.

2 Eventually the gradient eases over a lip, and the path runs left into a high basin. Step across a burn and slant up the hollow. Ascend the path to where it divides before the next burn; one branch going up steeply beside it and the other crossing it and winding rather less steeply up the moor. Both paths are wet and worn, and they meet again beyond the next lip, in a larger flat area. Climb the headwall at the back, the last scramble through the break in the rampart of cliffs, then slant left across the hillside and along a wide grassy shelf, which slopes upwards.

3 Cross a burn and go with the path as it soon swings right across the slope, then back again in a wide zigzag. From now on follow the cliff edge until you reach the summit, where the trig point is perched neatly with cliffs on three sides. It is like the prow of a ship, sailing north. If you are lucky you may see an eagle from here, gliding past below you in the sunshine. The view is superb, to all points of the compass.

Walk 24

Golden Eagle

4 Return by the route of ascent. If the day is still young and you are feeling energetic and do not mind road walking, take a small path that goes off on the left, just after crossing the first burn on the way down. It keeps to the edge of the cliffs and runs for about 1¼ miles/2 km descending gently. Then take a path that crosses a burn above a fine waterfall and goes down beside it, coming out through cottages to the road near the broch, Dun Dornaigil. It is about 1¼ miles/2km back up the road to the car park.

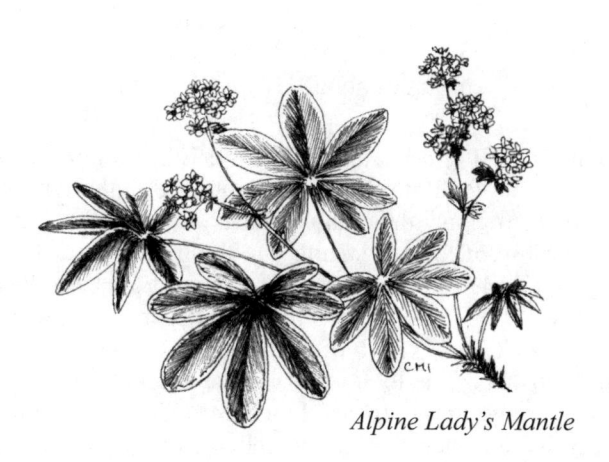

Alpine Lady's Mantle

Practicals

Type of walk: An excellent climb up a splendid hill. The path is mostly clear though it can be wet in places. The walk along the cliff edge gives fantastic views. If you take the longer route down you will have a 1¼ miles/2km road walk back to the car park, but it is a narrow quiet road.

Total distance: 5 miles/8km or 7 ½miles/12km if you take the longer option.

Time: 5 hours or 7 hours

Maps: OS Explorer 447/Landranger 9

25

The Wheelhouse, Loch Eriboll

Parking is limited near the start of this walk. There is room for one car by the telephone box at Laid, grid reference 416595, and for another 55yds/50m north in a little space. Otherwise there is plenty of room in various quarry entrances about 110yds/100m to 550yds/500m further on.

Loch Eriboll is a beautiful 10 mile/16km long sea loch running south from the Pentland Firth deep into the Sutherland hills. On the west side the rock is inhospitable quartzite, and this is where the clearance township of Laid is strung out along the shore. The east side is green and fertile with extensive outcrops of Durness limestone, and here there is one large farm. On a small peninsula across a dorlinn there is a large lime kiln built into the cliff. Mountain avens abound by the roadsides. The loch is very deep and has been used as a sheltered anchorage for centuries. During the Second World War British warships were sometimes stationed here, and the German U-boat fleet surrendered here in 1945.

Eriboll Wheelhouse

The **Wheelhouse** is an ancient homestead, so called because the arrangement of stone rafters inside look like the spokes of a wheel, radiating from a central ring of pillars with cross stones. Much of this building is still standing; the outer walls are about 6ft/2m high, there is a lintel over the entrance, many of the stones which supported the roof are there and even some of the roof, which is composed of large stone slabs.

1 Walk back to the track, which leaves the road by the telephone box, and follow it uphill until it makes a large bend and begins to go down again. Leave it and carry on in the same direction uphill to come to the side of a burn. Here there is a small path, not always very distinct, along the bank, and up great quartzite slabs that give very easy walking. The burn is delightful, a series of waterfalls and slides over quartzite steps and boiler plates. Turn round from time to time to admire the splendid view of Loch Eriboll. You may hear golden plover as you go higher; look for them standing on tussocks on the skyline.

2 Shortly before you reach a burn junction the path bears right, now marked by small quartzite stones standing on end at frequent intervals, and the occasional cairn. Cross the tributary burn and follow the markers up onto a stone-strewn hilltop. There is a small loch beyond it and a good view left to Beinn Spionnaidh. Bearberry and prostrate juniper grow among the stones; although only 920ft/280m above sea level the vegetation resembles mountain-top tundra.

Walk 25

3 Wander along the escarpment, still following vertical stone markers and using the wide slabs to walk on. Suddenly you become aware of the wheelhouse, a small round building tucked in below the crest of the escarpment on the north-west edge. Make your way over to it and enjoy your visit.

4 The easiest way back is to retrace your steps, but for variety continue down into the shallow valley beyond the

91

wheelhouse. Climb up again and walk along the side of a chain of three lochans where you may see greenshank. The view over to Whiten Head is fine. At the end of the third lochan wind right out of the little valley, rounding some large boulders, and descend quite steeply into another high valley. Keep along the side so as to avoid bog in the bottom. Walk south through this valley to a lip at the far end, then keep left to walk along a stony ridge. Eventually you have to cross the hillside so pick your way down with care; it is not difficult but can be wet and is a bit rough. Head in the direction of a hill with a sloping summit called An Lean-charn, on the far side of Loch Eriboll. To reward you for your effort the views are magnificent.

5 On reaching your outward track, turn left and return to your car. (If you parked further north along the road in one of the old quarry entrances you could head more to the left as you come down to reduce the road walking.)

Golden plover

Practicals

Type of walk: Interesting with splendid views. The paths are small but fairly clear and much of the way up is on quartzite slabs, lovely to walk on when dry but can be slippery when wet. The return across the hillside is pathless.

Total distance: 4 miles/6.5km
Time: 2–3 hours
Maps: OS Explorer 446/Landranger 9

One of the best walks we've done for ages! Sunshine, puffy white clouds, wonderful beaches, amazing inland sand dunes, fabulous views, wild flowers in abundance.... I'd love to come again! 24/8/11

Faraid Head

Park in the car park at Balnakeil Bay, grid reference 392688. To reach this, turn west in Durness and drive down past the craft village and on to the end of the road.

The **parish church at Balnakeil** was built in 1619 on the site of a much older church believed to have been built in the 8th century by St Maelrubha. The 17th century church is a ruin, now roofless and ivy-clad, having been in use until about 1814. A skull and crossbones within the church marks the tomb of Donald Macmurchow, a

Balnakeil Church

highwayman, who had murdered 18 people. In later life he funded the church, generously, in return for being buried there. The churchyard also contains the mass grave of the crew of a ship that sank off Faraid Head, with the loss of all hands, in 1849.

Sand couch grass and lyme grass are pioneer species on newly forming **dunes**. They are salt tolerant and can grow closer to the sea than most grasses. These two stabilise the dunes with their roots. They bind the sand in one place and this provides a wind break for more sand to be deposited. Marram grass can then take over. It is less tolerant of salt water. It grows fast and can keep pace with the sand being deposited and survive. It also spreads sideways, trapping the sand and keeping it in place. The sand dunes seen on this walk are very dramatic. Behind them lies the **machair**, an area of grassland enriched by wind blown sand where grow an abundance of wild flowers.

Walk 26

1 Walk down on to the wonderful clean firm sand and continue along to the end where there is a rock outcrop. At low tide you can get round this on the beach, but if the tide is too high go up the road where it leaves the beach and winds into the dunes. Pass through a gate in a wall and carry on until the road bends right to go inland.

2 Here find a way, with care, down through the dunes and back onto the beach. The views across the Kyle of Durness are stunning in all directions. At the end of the sand find a way up onto the grass and walk along above the low cliffs. They become higher as you go. Keep a sharp look-out in May and June for the

tiny deep pink Scottish primrose which does grow here in the short turf but is not common. There are also spring squills, heath spotted orchids and thyme. The cliffs become higher as you go north-west, until you end up on a narrow peninsula with sea crashing in on three sides. There is a fine view of more cliffs to the north-east. Fulmars soar overhead, out to sea gannets dive, and a constant stream of kittiwakes and guillemots pass low over the water.

3 Return from the peninsula and then bear east along the other (northern) end of the head. Climb up the next hill to follow the cliff round. From the hollow beyond it you can see rows of guillemots on the lower ledges, and fulmars nestled in higher up. Then climb up to join the road. Turn left and walk up to the next corner. Here you see the fence of the MoD establishment. You can go no further. Turn right and walk along below the fence, heading for a hill with a fine cairn on top. Climb it and continue over the ridge to the cliffs on the east side of the head. There are some fine stacks here, and views of the coast out to Whiten Head.

4 Walk right along the cliff edge, then follow a track down into the sand dunes. It is something of a switchback, but eventually you come out again on another cliff top with more fine views, the path running along a safe distance from the edge. Where the dunes start again, turn right and go downhill towards a sheep feeding area in a bowl of sand. Keep to the left and follow the obvious track through the dunes and sand; this eventually turns out to be the road. Keep on it to the gate and then down onto the sand at Balnakeil beach. Walk along the lovely bay to return to your car.

Razorbills

Practicals

Type of walk: A fine beach and cliff-top walk; the walking is easy although there are few paths.

Total distance: 5 miles/8km
Time: 3 hours
Maps: OS Explorer 446/Landranger 9

27

Sandwood Bay

Park in the large car park at Blairmore, grid reference 195600. Access this by driving along the B801 from Rhiconich to Kinlochbervie then taking the minor road right for Oldshoremore. Continue to Blairmore.

Sandwood Bay is generally considered to be the finest of many splendid bays on the west coast of Sutherland. It is wide and at least a mile long, maybe as much as two miles at low tide when the sand continues beyond the northern cliffs. Sand dunes fringe it on the inland side, with a large freshwater loch behind. A short river flows from the loch through the dunes and across the beach near its north end; it is quite wide but can be easily forded. At the southern end of the bay is a dramatic red sandstone stack called **Am Buachaille**, the Shepherd or Herdsman, standing on a rocky plinth just off shore.

The **John Muir Trust**, named after the Scottish conservationist John Muir, owns Sandwood Bay and much land in the area. It is a charity devoted to the conservation of

Sandwood Bay

wild land in Scotland. In addition to owning land it also works closely with groups of crofters, such as the Assynt Crofters' Trust, who have bought their land and wish to manage it sustainably.

1 Cross the road and walk up the track signed to Sandwood beside a cottage. Go through a kissing gate beside a field gate; there is a sign asking you to keep dogs on a close lead for the safety of lambs and of ground nesting birds. The track runs along above a loch, where you may see greylag geese, then leaves the fields and goes over moorland. Walk past another large loch, Loch na Gainimh, on the left. Towards the end of this loch look for a small footpath on the left, which cuts a corner. Otherwise go on to take an obvious left branch of the track. The footpath soon joins it. On a good day, in spring or summer, the air is loud with skylarks, and you may hear the plaintive calls of golden plover. Go past a small lochan on the right, then downhill to pass a large one, Loch a'Mhuillin, on the left. Bonxies (great skuas) nest on the moorland and if you are very lucky you could see a short-eared owl. Look for red-throated divers on the lochs.

2 The track now becomes a path, quite eroded in places although a lot of work has been done on the drainage. Go past two more lochs on the right and then come over a brow to see Sandwood Loch below, and the ruined house. A little further on the bay comes into view; it is breathtaking. There are lines of cliffs, with the top of Cape Wrath lighthouse just peeping over the farthest one. Go down the path through the dunes and out onto the bay. You will want to spend a lot of time here. There are outcrops of rocks in the middle and as you go down, the splendid stack Am Buachaille comes into view at the south end of the bay. Botanically inclined walkers may like to wander over to the north end of the bay, fording the river, and climbing the grass and rocks at the far side,

or go round the end into the next bay at low tide. There are carpets of 'lime-lovers' such as mountain avens, and in places, moss campion; the rock appears to be gneiss but either there is some Durness limestone there too or the soil is modified by blown shell sand. Out to sea look for gannets, terns and kittiwakes and you may see arctic skuas and bonxies.

3 When you have finished exploring, you can return by your outward path – this is quickest. But if you feel more adventurous go to the south end of the beach and climb up a path slanting steeply up the sand dunes. Soon you leave the sand for short turf and the path becomes easier, although very close to the edge of the cliff in places and quite exposed. Keep on up to reach the cliff top above Am Buachaille. Admire its situation on a fine plinth of sandstone.

Arctic Skua (dark phase)

4 Carry on round the cliffs. The path is small but obviously well-used. Be careful as you go through an area of collapsed caves and chasms. Then cross a burn and climb a little to look down into a deep valley with a small stack on the rocks at its mouth. Here the path turns away from the sea and runs downhill, inland. It crosses a boggy area and then continues along the edge of the steep bank above the burn. It now follows the burn and a fence to Loch A'Mhuillin. Walk round the left side to rejoin your outward path. Enjoy the splendid view ahead of Ben Stack, Arkle, Foinaven, Cranstackie and Ben Spionnaidh.

Practicals

Type of walk: A long walk. The track is distinct and mostly good though somewhat eroded in places. The cliff path is small and quite exposed at first but gives wonderful views. It is quite boggy going back up the valley to Loch a'Mhuillin. Leave plenty of time to enjoy the bay.

Total distance: 8 miles/13km if you return the same way.
9 miles/14.5km if you feel more adventurous.
Time: 5 hours or 6 hours
Maps: OS Explorer 446/Landranger 9

28

Polin and Oldshoremore

Park down by the little pier at Droman, grid reference 186593. To get there take the B801 from Rhiconich to Kinlochbervie and then turn right on a minor road to Oldshoremore. Carry on until you pass the large car park for Sandwood Bay at Blairmore, then take the next left turn to Droman.

Beyond Kinlochbervie, **Loch Inchard** opens out, and there are wide views across to the mountains further south. There are several small scattered crofting communities here and two magnificent sandy bays at Polin and Oldshoremore. Much of this area now belongs to the John Muir Trust.

Polin Bay and Ben Stack

Walk 28

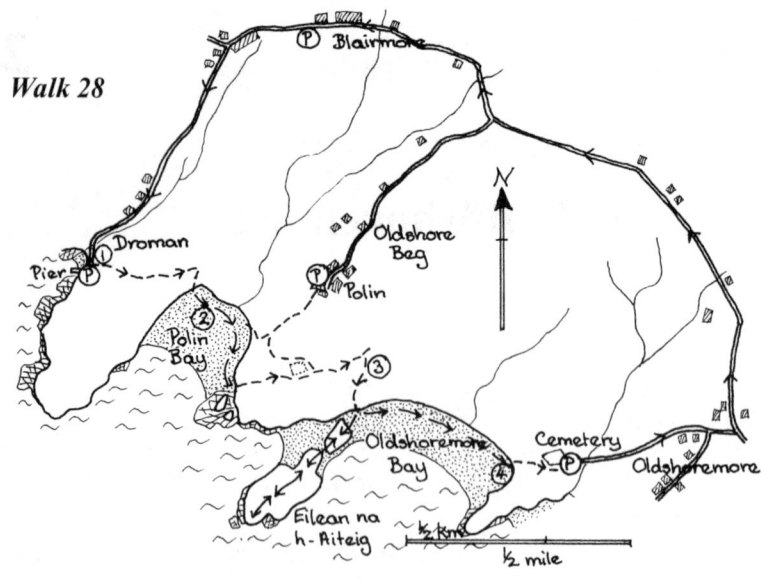

1 Admire the fine cliffs and attractive small bay at Droman. There are many rock doves here, and sandpipers and oystercatchers call. In the field by the car park are carpets of kingcups and northern marsh orchids. Walk uphill away from the car park following a signpost to Polin Beach. The path runs beside a fence, a wall and then a fence again where there is a stile to climb. It then swings away to the left, turns back right and comes down by the remains of a fence to Polin Beach. This is a magnificent bay of white sand curving between cliffs at either end. It is completely unspoiled.

2 Cross the bay and walk out round the low cliffs at the far (south) side. Where the sand ends, go left across boulders and climb easily up a grassy gully on a small path. At the top, head for an ancient field enclosure and walk through it to pick up a distinct small path at the far left hand corner. If the tide is high and you cannot get round the low cliffs, climb up sloping rocks near the end of the beach to find a path running along through the marram outside a fence. Follow this to a low board to block the way to sheep, which you step over, then immediately turn right and wind round above a tiny burn. Go through a gateway and cross the next field on a fairly distinct path. At the far side negotiate a ruinous fence and bear left to join the other path at the end of the ancient enclosure. Go round a rocky mound to cross a grassy area on a raised way. Pass through a shallow ravine. Beyond this, the path drops down across turf studded with pansies and heath spotted orchids and contours round the hillside, with a stunning view across

the white sands and turquoise sea of Oldshoremore Bay to Foinaven, Arkle and Ben Stack. Look for terns, divers, and shags on the water.

3   Where three lines of old wall remnants run down the hillside, turn right and follow the third one to a stile over the full-sized wall. Head slightly right beyond it to go down easy grass slopes. At the bottom is a rock step which you must scramble down; it looks tricky but is actually easy. There is a tidal island to your right and if you wish you can cross over to it. Climb the sloping rocks to gain access to a path, which runs along to cliffs at the end. Enjoy exploring but keep an eye on the tide. Then return from the island and enjoy the stroll along the wide beautiful beach.

4   At the far end there are two obvious paths leading up off the sand. Take the first left, which leads to wooden steps through the dunes to the top of the low cliff. Go through a kissing gate and follow the path downhill to the cemetery car park. If you wish to go out to the headland, turn right before the kissing gate. Either return the way you came, or be met, or walk back along the road. To do the latter follow the road up into the village of Oldshoremore, turning left where another road comes in, then left again at the main road. Go past the road down to Oldshorebeg and Polin, then uphill to pass the car park at Blairmore and turn left downhill to Droman.

Northern Marsh Orchid

Practicals

Type of walk: A lovely walk with the best part along the shore on the sand and the small paths. The road is narrow and not very busy, but even so you may well prefer to retrace your steps along the coast.

Total distance: 3 miles/5km there and back along the beach. 5 miles/8km if returning by the road.
Time: 1½ hours/2½ hours
Maps: OS Explorer 446/Landranger 9

29

Loch na Tuadh, between Arkle and Foinaven

Park in the car park at the Loch Stack Lodge road end, grid reference 269435; it can take 6 cars and 7 if well parked. If full, drive 220yds/200m north-west where there is also some room by an old cottage. To access this area, drive 3 miles/5km south-east along the A838 from Laxford Bridge.

Arkle and **Foinaven** are two most spectacular mountains in this wild and rugged part of the country. They are both Corbetts, although Foinaven is only just below Munro height. They are both composed of sharp angular quartzite which forms craggy spurs and huge grey scree slopes. Foinaven has a long narrow ridge and dramatic corries on the north-east side; Arkle is smaller but its equally narrow ridge wraps round a corrie above Loch na Tuadh. Both mountains gave names to racehorses belonging to the Duke of Westminster.

Loch na Tuadh

1 Walk down the private road towards Loch Stack Lodge. Cross the bridge over the River Laxford and turn right on an unpaved track which runs along above Loch Stack. You may see black-throated divers here in spring and summer. The track soon swings away and runs up by a burn which it crosses and continues on the other side. There are waterlilies and bogbean in the slower flowing parts of the burn, and dragonflies patrol their territories in summer. The path leaves the burn and climbs over a ridge to descend with a loch to the right. It is worth looking over all these lochs to see red-throated divers, or wigeon, or possibly greenshank. Carry on between two more lochs, with the vast bulk of Arkle towering in front, to turn left where the path makes an abrupt right-angled bend.

2 Carry on above Loch Airigh a'Bhaird and then wind round at the foot of the steep ground, which is the beginning of Arkle. Away to your left a loch comes into view, then cottages on Loch Inchard and finally the sea. Climb gently and then descend into the wide valley between Arkle and Foinaven. From now on Foinaven dominates the landscape.

Walk 29

3 The track comes down to a wide shallow river flowing out of Loch na Tuadh. Cross on stepping stones. These are fairly easy but some are quite widely spaced and some are an awkward shape. If you feel you can't manage them, or if the river is in spate, there is a small path that runs along

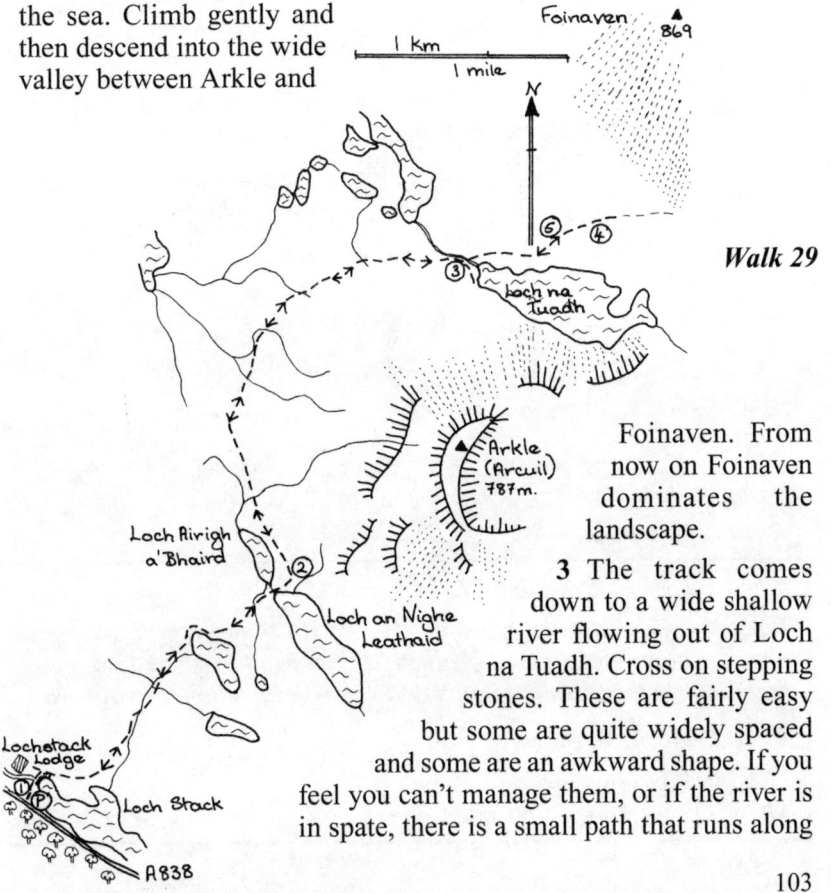

the near bank to Loch na Tuadh; it is worth going on to the loch for the view. To continue, cross and go along the track. The view becomes more dramatic with every step. There is an upper corrie (also with a loch) beyond Loch na Tuadh but the track you are on peters out below the screes of Foinaven. You can easily walk into the upper corrie but it is pathless and you will have to make your own way.

4 You can see the waterfalls coming in from below the Bealach Horn, and Meall nan Horn beyond. To your right, towers Arkle and to the left, Foinaven. Go as far as you wish. You may like to go down to the bouldery loch shore, where there are common sandpipers. There are stonechats in the heather and you may hear a cuckoo calling.

5 When you can tear yourself away from this amazing place, return the way you came. Enjoy the different views, with first the high gneiss moorland spangled with lochs, then as you round a corner the neat cone of Ben Stack comes into view.

Greenshank

Practicals

Type of walk: A distinct track all the way. In some conditions the stepping stones might be a problem. If you want to go on into the inner corrie there are no paths and you will have to pick your way.

Total distance: 10 miles/16.5km

Time: 5–6 hours

Maps: OS Explorer 445/Landranger 9

30

Handa Island

Park in the car park behind the shore at Tarbet, grid reference 164488. To access this, turn west off the A894 about three miles north of Scourie. The road is signed to Tarbet, Foindle and Fanagmore, and to Handa Ferry (Passengers only). Keep left at the road junction. It is a typical small Sutherland road, full of hills and abrupt bends, so drive with care.

The Great Stack, Handa

The **ferry** runs every day except Sundays, taking 10 people at a time, from 9am to 2 pm. After that it brings people back. The last ferry return is officially at 5 pm but as long as you have reached the beach well before five they won't leave you. However you should not be late back to the beach.

Handa is privately owned by Dr. Jean Balfour and the Scourie Estate, but is managed for its magnificent wildlife by the Scottish Wildlife Trust. There were eight families living in the village above the visitor centre until 1847. The islanders had a parliament, similar to St Kilda, which met daily and the oldest widow was considered the Queen. The year 1847 was the year of the potato famine and the islanders asked to be evacuated and took ship for Canada from Laxford Bridge. The island then became a sheep walk.

A **warden** will meet you on the beach and lead you along a path through the dunes to a small hut or visitor centre, where he will give you a short talk about the island and provide you with a map.

1 Leave the hut by the grassy path behind it, from where you should look back to admire the white sand beaches. Climb gently to a gate through a fence then wind round the hillside between the ruins of the old village. Look left to see the land the people cultivated; strips with oats and potatoes. You may hear snipe and sedge warbler here.

2 At a fork in the path go left, winding along well above the shoreline. Soon the path becomes a boardwalk. There are bluebells and primroses in sheltered areas, and mauve and white heath spotted orchids in the moorland. Look out for arctic skuas, more delicate than the ubiquitous great skua or bonxie. Eiders coo in the bays and terns scream overhead, and occasionally you might see a red-throated diver.

3 The path winds round to the right nearer to the shore, with places where you can go out onto promontories and get good views of nesting guillemots and razorbills. Fulmars soar past on stiff wings, curious as ever about people on the cliff top. Walk out onto the headland of Meall a'Bhodha, which will eventually become detached and form a stack. Then return to the main path and climb steadily. The next feature is a huge hole called Poll Ghlup where the roof of a cave has collapsed. There is a low arch at the base leading out to the sea. The cliffs overhang here and are unsafe. Climb up the cliff path again to reach the highest point of the spectacular cliffs with their rows of guillemots. Towards the top of the cliffs you may see puffins if you look carefully.

4 Walk past a small lochan and then follow a side path downhill towards the Great Stack. This is crowded with guillemots and razorbills, with puffins in the vegetated areas on top. Admire the spectacle and return to the main path. It goes round the head of a deep geo with the Great Stack across the entrance. Walk downhill to the head of Puffin Bay where you turn right. Ahead is a small lochan where you may see a large number of bonxies bathing. Continue down the path across the centre of the island to reach the junction where you turned left on the way out. Carry on through the old village and down to the visitor shelter, then over to the landing beach. If it is busy you may have to wait a while for a place in the boat so leave plenty of time.

Puffins

Practicals

Type of walk: Good paths often with duck-boarding.

Total distance: 4 miles/6.5km
Time: 3 hours but leave time to enjoy the birds and the superb cliff scenery.
Maps: OS Explorer 445/Landranger 9

31

Kylestrome and Loch Glendhu

Park in the car park at Kylestrome, grid reference 218346. Access this by crossing the new bridge at Kylesku to the north side and, in ½ mile/1km, turn right down a minor road, then immediately right again into the car park.

In the shooting season (July to the end of October) you are asked to contact the Reay Estate Office (just down the road) before going on the hill.

The **Stack of Glencoul** is the distinctive mountain at the head of Loch Glencoul, the more southerly of the two lochs which meet at Kylesku. It is famous in geological circles for the obvious fault, part of the Moine Thrust Zone, which runs across it below the summit. In certain light conditions this stands out clearly.

The **Moine Thrust Fault** formed when two ancient continents collided, pushing one up over the other so that the Moine rocks on top are actually much older than the rocks they are resting on.

Quinag and Kylesku Bridge

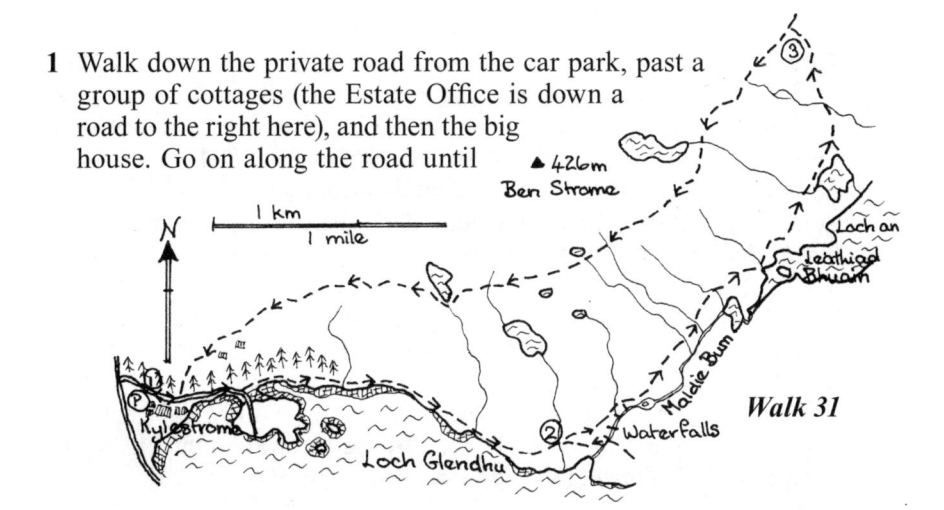

1 Walk down the private road from the car park, past a group of cottages (the Estate Office is down a road to the right here), and then the big house. Go on along the road until

Walk 31

Terns

the point where it crosses to an island and take a track on the left which follows the loch shore. At first the track runs through conifers, where you may see siskins, then out into open country. Look across to the islands to see numbers of seals hauled out on the rocks. Red-throated divers and terns can be seen on and over the water.

2 After 2 miles/3.4km the track comes to a junction. Take the right branch and walk downhill to the bridge over the Maldie Burn. Do not cross, but walk a few yards up the bank towards a small turbine house, until there is a view of the fine waterfall. Then return to the path, turn right, walk up to the junction and turn right again, climbing the valley side above the turbulent burn. A higher waterfall comes into view, with a small weir above it and the start of the pipeline to the turbine house. As you climb, look back from time to time at the fantastic view. Then a small loch appears on the right. Carry on up to reach the larger Loch an Leathiad Bhuain and then walk along its side, climbing gently but steadily. Look for black-throated divers on the water in summer. The view ahead opens out. The path curves left with a burn to the right and goes up to join another path.

3 Turn left here. This track was an old stalkers' path, but has been 'upgraded' to a landrover track, and at present is quite difficult to walk. With luck it will settle down in time. The amazing views compensate for any difficulty, but stand still to look at them. The track winds round high above the valley, passing a small lochan on the right, and the view opens up over Lochs Glendhu and Glencoul to Quinag and the Stack of Glencoul. The track descends very steeply here and is loose and it is easier, where possible, to use loops of the old stalkers' track, which is gentler and zigzags. Wind round another loch, and then begin to descend towards a cottage, pastures and woods. Come down by a deer fence to a main track and cross. A sign here says that if stalking is in progress they will show a red disc. Carry on down the track into conifers and rejoin the outward road by the gateway to the big house. Turn right and return to the car park.

Red-throated diver

Practicals

Type of walk: The views are superb. The outward track is fine but the upper track has been newly made to replace an old stalkers' path and at the time of writing it has not settled down and is rough. However it is dry.

Total distance: 8 miles/13km

Time: 4–5 hours

Maps: OS Explorers 442 and 445/Landranger 15

32

Eas a'Chual Aluinn

Park in the car park towards the top of the hill, south of Kylesku, grid reference 240292. There are 3 unsurfaced parking places further on up the hill.

Eas a'Chual Aluinn, the beautiful waterfall of Coul, is reputed to be the highest in Britain. It is about 650ft/277m high and consists of three consecutive falls followed by a waterslide.

There is a story that tells of a young girl who was required to marry a man whom she hated. She hid on the steep wooded cliffs called Leitir Dhubh. Unfortunately she was discovered but rather than submit to the marriage she flung herself off the cliff. It is said that the waterfall was formed by her streaming hair and is sometimes called **'the Maiden's Tresses'**.

1 Walk on up the A-road, for a few steps, to the old road and take a vague path, left, towards Loch na Gainmhich. Look for red-throated divers here in spring and

Eas a'Chual Aluinn

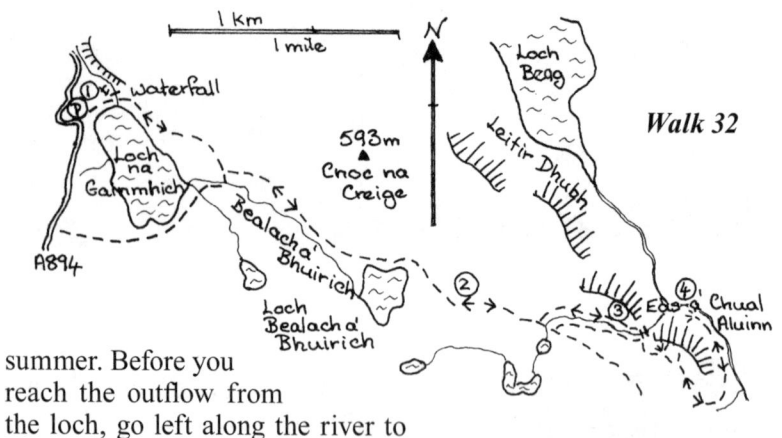

Walk 32

summer. Before you reach the outflow from the loch, go left along the river to see a pleasing waterfall. Return along the river and cross it by stepping stones and a part of a dam. Go up the bank at the far side (do not continue along the loch shore) and contour well above the water. It is quite wet in places but good boots help you along. Climb gradually above the loch to its end. Join a path which comes round from the other side of the loch, and continue climbing ahead, now on a stony stalkers' path which then runs along the north side of a depression in the hills. The land is all lumps and bumps, called 'cnoc and lochan country', with Glas Bheinn towering over to the south. Climb again to see, over the next lip, Loch Bealach a'Bhuirich, cradled in a hollow of the hills. Follow the path as it contours above the water, then climbs again out of this bowl to the highest point of the walk at the Bealach a' Bhuirich. Yellow mountain saxifrage lines the sides of many burns and wet places. The view is splendid with the Stack of Glencoul and Beinn Leoid in front and, off to the right, a string of lochs in Glen Cassley. To the left you can just see Arkle.

2 Descend the path which goes in a wide sweep round the high bowl in front. The burn responsible for the waterfall, Eas a'Chual Aluinn, is now obvious to your right. Wind down until you have to ford this burn. There are paths down both sides and they are both eroded and peaty in places, but it is probably best to stay on the side you are on. It depends whether you want to cross the burn high up or would rather do it lower down; both need care but neither is likely to be too difficult.

3 Eventually you reach the fall. In order to see it at all you have to cross the burn to the south side and then carry on along a rough path down to the right; it is quite steep in places but can be negotiated with care. This will bring you to a lower ridge with several viewing points from which you can see the whole of the top fall and a bit of the second, but

the cliff is too steep to allow more. Most people will be content with this but if you are a waterfall enthusiast and have plenty of time, walk south along a valley which develops between the ridge and the main hill. Keep left; there is no proper path and you have to make your own way over rough ground but it is surprisingly easy. Make use of a deer path as it winds round to the left and slants down towards the main valley bottom. Keep as high as you can below the cliffs and make for a small promontory, from which you have a splendid view of the full length of the fall, three drops and a waterslide.

4 Now you have to climb all the way back up again, then retrace your steps over the high bealach, enjoying the fine views of Quinag and Edrachillis Bay. Come down the long slope to reach your car.

Yellow mountain saxifrage

Practicals

Type of walk: This is a long walk into wild country. As far as the top of the waterfall the paths are clear and mostly good stalkers' paths. If you want to make your way down into the valley to see the entire fall there are only deer tracks and you need to have some ability to find your way across pathless country. Do not attempt to do this in mist. Take great care around the top of the fall, especially with children.

Stalking takes place in this area and the telephone number given is 01571 822242, or the Assynt Estate Office 01571 844203.

Total distance: 7 miles/11.4km. Add on an extra 2 miles/3.4km if you go down into the valley.

Time: 3–4 hours, or 4–5 if you go down to the valley.

Maps: OS Explorer 442/Landranger 15

33

Spidean Coinich, Quinag

Park in a large space in the old quarry, on the east side, near the summit of the road, the A894, from Skiag Bridge to Kylesku, grid reference 233274.

Quinag is the most northerly of the Torridon sandstone hills which stretch up the west coast from Applecross. It is a complex massif with three main summits, all Corbetts, which means that there is a drop of at least 500ft/152m between each of them. Quinag forms a rough Y-shape; the two northern arms, Sail Gorm and Sail Garbh above Kylesku, are buttressed with dramatic cliffs, but the southern arm, Spidean Coinich, slopes gently up from Skiag Bridge. It is easy to climb all three summits from the Bealach a'Chornaidh at the centre of the massif, although this walk only goes up the most southerly.

Spidean Coinich, Quinag

1 Cross the road and take the stalkers' path over the footbridge and on across the moor. Ignore a path on your left (your return route) and carry on the good path as it climbs towards the corrie. It bends right to keep to the high ground; then the surfaced path ends and a rough walkers' path continues. Cross a burn on easy stones. As the path climbs higher the loch in the corrie comes into view, below dramatic cliffs on Spidean Coinich. You may see red-throated divers on the water in summer, especially early in the morning. The path continues well to the right of the loch, climbing easily towards the Bealach a'Chornaidh, which is at the centre of the Quinag massif. Cross a high alp where there are several springs, your last chance to get water for some time. When you reach the bealach, pause and enjoy the magnificent view south and west.

2 Climb the steep footpath up the ridge to your left. It is quite loose in places but zigzags and there is no real difficulty until it arrives at the crest of a narrow ridge and turns left along it. This is very straightforward but narrow and airy and may not suit people who have no head for heights. In a few places you have to use your hands. On reaching the top of an intermediate summit, Creag na h'Iolaire Ard, the ridge broadens, and here pause to admire the fantastic view. Descend easily to a col and climb the last rocky stretch on quartzite to the summit of Spidean Coinich. There are several cairns and a wide rocky top. The view encompasses Foinaven and Arkle to the north, round to Ben More Assynt and Conival to the east and Loch Assynt below, with Cul Mor and Suilven and more hills into the far distance, then the island-studded sea with Skye to the south and the hills of Harris.

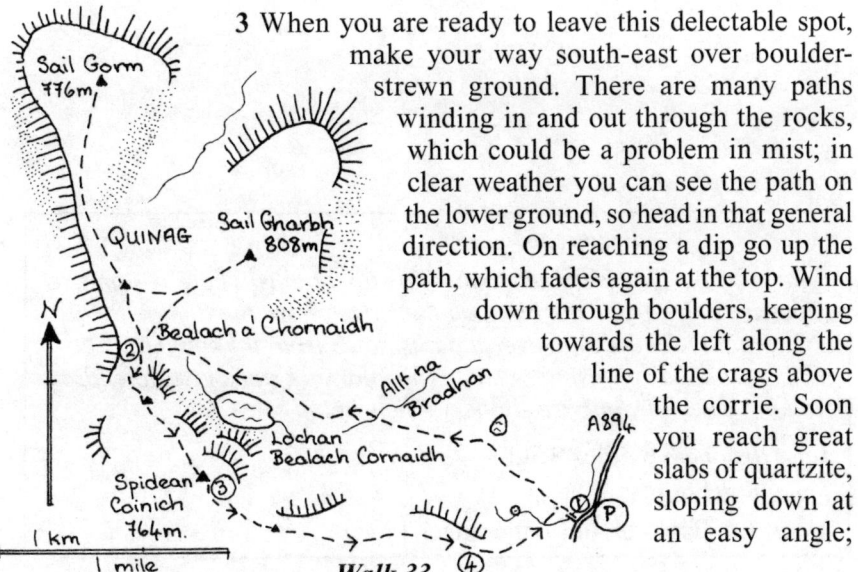

3 When you are ready to leave this delectable spot, make your way south-east over boulder-strewn ground. There are many paths winding in and out through the rocks, which could be a problem in mist; in clear weather you can see the path on the lower ground, so head in that general direction. On reaching a dip go up the path, which fades again at the top. Wind down through boulders, keeping towards the left along the line of the crags above the corrie. Soon you reach great slabs of quartzite, sloping down at an easy angle;

Walk 33

walk on these wherever possible, although bear in mind that they are slippery when wet. Follow the path between them, linking them together. As you go listen for golden plovers in spring and summer.

4 Towards the bottom of the slope the quartzite slabs come to an end and the path becomes peaty and boggy in places. Cross a burn and at the junction with your outward path, turn right, cross the bridge and walk back to the car park.

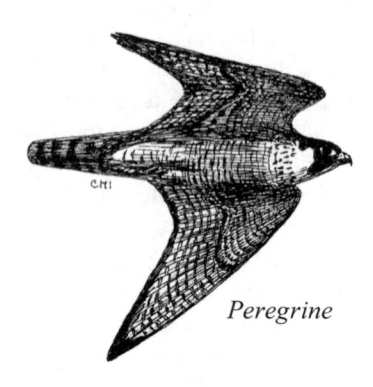

Peregrine

Practicals

Type of walk: This is a fine climb on distinct paths. There is some exposure and easy scrambling on the ridge above the Bealach a'Chornaidh. There are several paths down from the summit, which could be confusing in mist. The quartzite slabs give splendid walking when dry but are slippery when wet.

Total distance: 6 miles/9.5km.

Time: 5–6 hours

Maps: OS Explorer 442/Landranger 15

34

Drumbeg Peat Roads

Park in the car park at the Drumbeg Viewpoint, grid reference 120330. This is reached by the B869 which runs, tortuously, from Lochinver to Unapool near Kylesku.

Dogs allowed on this walk only on leads.

The **peat roads** were built for the crofters of Drumbeg and Culkein Drumbeg to gain access to their peat cuttings and transport the peats out. They have been there for more than 150 years. Between 1890 and 1914 work was carried out by local people to improve them with funding from the Congested Districts Board.

Except for the Outer Hebrides (Western Isles) the Assynt landscape is like nowhere else in Britain. The basic rock is **Lewisian Gneiss** which is the oldest rock in Britain. It has been eroded and now forms a lumpy landscape, full of knolls and hollows, often referred to as 'cnoc

Loch Bad an Og and Quinag

117

and lochan'. On top of this are mountains of Torridon sandstone which rear up in strange abrupt shapes. The effect is magnificent and brings many walkers to visit Assynt.

In 1992 the **North Assynt Estate** was put up for sale, as 'wild' land. In fact it is quite largely crofted. The crofters, tired of landowners who were not interested and even negligent, formed the Assynt Crofters Trust. This gained wide-spread support, and in 1993 it succeeded in buying the land. This was the first of several community buy-outs in the Highlands of Scotland.

Walk 34

1 Before you leave the car park, admire the splendid view over Edrachillis Bay to the mountains of the far north. Then turn left, east, along the road. Walk past the excellent village shop and the pub until you can turn right on a narrow road signed for a tearoom. Pass through a kissing gate and then a gate and stroll down beside the tearoom. At the bottom of the hill go through two more gates on a lovely green track curving up and round a hill. It continues, well-made and well-maintained, through typical gneiss countryside, full of rocky lumps and hollows. As you round a corner, look for a small lochan on your left, then there is a larger one, sparkling blue, to your right. Suddenly there is a small one on the left near to the track, pleasantly fringed with birch trees, softening the view. The next lochan is a tiny pool on the right.

2 Climb on up the track to the crest of the hill, from where there is a fine view of the continuing track, which passes another reedy loch and goes on below grassy hillsides, an oasis in the rather bleak vegetation, beyond. The dramatic shapes of Suilven and Canisp tower in the distance. Look for a small cairn on the right of the track just after the track begins to descend. This marks the start of a small but distinct path,

through the heather, contouring the lumps and bumps with the reedy loch down below on the left. Follow the path down to a new fence to climb a small stile. Beyond, cross a small burn then follow the path as it winds right and runs below a steep hillside. To your right is a shallow pool with common reed and bogbean.

3 The path winds left and rises gently to join another old track (this is the Culkein Drumbeg Peat Road) at another small cairn. Walk on through a gate then wind right. Stop to admire the superb view; now with Quinag as well as Suilven and Canisp. The track winds left again and soon enters a low birch wood. There is another loch, Loch Bad an Og, to the right, well seen as the path climbs. Look for dabchicks in the reeds. Carry on through less wooded areas with some fine glimpses of the sea and Quinag, towering away to the right, until Loch Drumbeg appears on the right. The path slopes down almost to water level, then crosses a burn and runs slightly uphill past a caravan to a gate onto the road.

4 Bear right and walk back to the car park, with good views to your right over Loch Drumbeg. There is little traffic and there are good verges in most places. You may see and hear common sandpipers by the loch as you go, in summer.

Dabchick

Practicals

Type of walk: Most enjoyable. On paths and tracks, with about a mile on a quiet road at the end.

Total distance: 4½ miles/7.4km
Time: 2–3 hours
Maps: OS Explorer 442/Landranger 15

35

The Old Man of Stoer

Park in the car park before the lighthouse, at the end of the public road, grid reference 004327. To access this, take the B869 north from Lochinver for 6 miles/9.4km to Stoer. Go past a cemetery and ruined church on your right as you climb the hill. About a mile further on turn left onto a minor road, signed to Point of Stoer. Ignore the first turning; carry on past the school to the next junction where you turn sharp left. Drive on to the end of the road.

The **Old Man** is a fine sea stack 200ft/62m high, on the west side of the peninsula close in to the cliffs. It was first climbed in 1966 by Tom Patey and Brian Robertson. Nowadays it is climbed more frequently and the top is hung with abseil slings.

The Old Man of Stoer

1 Walk ahead out of the car park, heading to the right of the lighthouse. A track comes down the hill from the right and where this joins the road there is a wide grassy path, signed to Point of Stoer. Climb easily up this path; it is mainly dry and grassy but there are a few wet places which you have to avoid. As the gradient eases look left to see a great slab of rock which has split away from the cliff. Look back from here to see the lighthouse perched dramatically above its cliff with churning waves below. Then walk on, slightly downhill.

2 After ½ mile/1 km from the start a steep-sided gully cuts right across the way. There are several paths down into it and out again but it is quite eroded on the south side. Walk along the edge, inland, until you find a path down which suits you. Then climb up the easier north side and cross the level ground beyond, heading gradually back towards the cliff top. You should see many seabirds, especially in spring and summer; both arctic and great skuas hunt here and kittiwakes, shags and black guillemots nest. Gannets dive out at sea. You may see seals below, and it is a great place to look for whales and dolphins. Follow the path along the cliff edge to reach a narrow promontory, from where you can see the Old Man of Stoer, a spectacular sea stack. Climb to the right above the cliffs then contour round the side of Sidhean Mor and finally descend quite steeply to the level area opposite the Old Man. You may see people climbing on it.

3 Go on over gentler ground to reach the Point of Stoer. From here turn south and walk above the cliffs on the other side, then climb easily up the end of Sidhean Mor to the trig point (528ft/161m); the view from here is stunning. Continue along

Walk 34

the top, keeping to the higher ground. Pass to the right of a small lochan, then carry on ahead towards the communications mast on Sidhean Beag. Before you reach it you should meet a track running downhill through some old wartime buildings. Turn right and walk back down to the car park.

Great Skua (bonxie)

Practicals

Type of walk: Exhilarating with fine cliff scenery. The path out to the Old Man is quite worn, especially the first part, and divides several times. Choose your preferred route. The return over Sidhean Mor is almost pathless but easy terrain for walking.

Total distance: 4 miles/6.5km
Time: 3 hours
Maps: OS Explorer 442/Landranger 15

36

Achmelvich to Alltanabradhan

Park in the large car park behind the beach at Achmelvich, grid reference 059249. To get there take the B869 which leaves the A837 one mile north of Lochinver. After 2 miles/3.4km take a minor road on the left signed to Achmelvich and Youth Hostel. The car park is clearly signed at the end of the public road, 2 miles/3.4km after the junction.

The Alltanabradhan Meal Mill is all that remains of a tiny building which used to grind the flour for the townships of Achmelvich and Clachtoll. It was of a type called a 'clack' mill, where the upper millstone was connected through the lower one to a horizontally-revolving paddle wheel turned by the 'fluim', a millrace through the centre of the building. The mill was in use from the 1600s to the late 1800s. You can still see the millrace, and there are several millstones lying on the ground.

Alltanabradhan Mill

123

Walk 36

1. Leave the car park in the direction of the beach, passing through a gate onto a track heading north, and signed to Alltanabradhan. Wind round on the track across the flowery machair, with glimpses of white sand to your left. There are early purple orchids in spring. Go through another gate and notice a lily lochan to your right, ahead. The track climbs slightly over a crest; there are several houses here. Take a signed footpath on the left which runs downhill to cross a burn, then climbs steeply up the other side. Join a path coming in front of a house and carry on up to the top of the hill, then down the other side. Go through a small gate in a wall and climb the far side of the valley, then cross a level area and descend again into another valley. Wind right and climb again. Look for stonechats and wheatears.

2. Over the next col come down to a wide white track, which is a private road to a group of holiday cottages. Bear left following the signs, then right to walk up the right branch of the track towards a large house. Keep left outside its gate and the well-made path carries on through a narrow defile. Go down steps to cross a burn on a bank of stones to a small ruin which was the meal mill. After exploring the tiny building, continue along the path as it runs seaward down the narrow glen. Go through a gap in a ruined wall and on to the grass behind the delightful sandy bay (at high tide much of the sand is covered). You may see mergansers and eiders here and terns screech overhead in summer. It is a lovely place for a picnic.

3. When you are ready to return, retrace your steps. Each time you climb out of a valley you will have a splendid view of Stac Pollaidh, Cul Beag and Cul Mor from the top. If you want to visit another

Early Purple Orchid

fine beach turn right after crossing the tiny burn below the group of houses nearest to Achmelvich and follow an indistinct path across the pasture and down to the sand. This is a magnificent white curving beach enclosed by low gneiss cliffs. You can return by the way you came or if you are happy rock scrambling go to the south end of the beach and climb up where it is obvious that everyone else does. Follow the narrow path at the top, before descending a rock step, easily done by sitting down. Slant up the sandy slope beyond, walk straight ahead and come out onto the machair behind Achmelvich Bay. Walk left to rejoin your outward route.

Merganser

Practicals

Type of walk: A delightful short walk on good paths (although the alternative return involves a little scrambling). The views are splendid, and the beaches superb.

Total distance: 3 miles/5km
Time: 2–3 hours
Maps: OS Explorer 442/Landranger 15

37

River Inver and Glen Canisp

Park in the centre of Lochinver where there are several car parks, using the one at grid reference 093226

Dubh Chlais once had 6 households, comprising 43 people altogether. They were cleared in 1800 to provide land for sheep, and today only the ruined walls of the houses and field enclosures remain.

Glencanisp Lodge was built in 1850 for the tenant farmer, and was later extended to become a shooting lodge. It is now community owned and has been run by the Assynt Foundation since 2005.

Lochinver is the largest village on the west coast of Sutherland. It was a major fishing port with its harbour thronged with boats from the east coast, especially on Thursdays when the fleet returned

Loch Druim Suardalain and Suilven

from four days at sea. The catch was almost entirely whitefish, unlike Ullapool to the south which specialised in herring. These days, however, there are few boats and the huge facility built with EU money is mostly empty. The main source of income now is tourism.

Walk 36

1. Walk back up the road to the new road bridge at the north end of the village. Go through a kissing gate onto the riverside path, which runs beside the River Inver through mature deciduous woodland. The river is spectacular in this first section, full of waterfalls and rapids. Look for dippers and grey wagtails. Paths down to the left lead to fishing stances. At a steep area there is a section of boardwalk and a fence; look around here for both beech and oak ferns. Beyond, take the right hand path at a junction, climbing steeply then levelling out to run along a terrace, then downhill again. Go through another kissing gate and into woodland with many Scots pine trees. Climb again through the beautiful woodland. The river below is a fisherman's playground, with many stances of various kinds and higher up, weirs and partial dams.

2. Eventually, leave the trees through a gate gap in a fence and soon cross a plank footbridge. Pass two fishing stances on the left and go round a bend to reach the end of a large island. At this point a path branches off on the right, leading up the side of a wide valley. Follow it as it climbs, crossing another burn on a plank footbridge and then winding through pleasant grassland. At the top of the first rise look for the ruins of old houses, the village of Dubh Chlais. Walk on to a deer fence and go through the metal kissing gate, turn right and wind uphill round the side of the valley. In May the gorse is magnificent. Go over the top of Druim Suardalain, where you suddenly have the most amazing view of Suilven and Canisp. Descend steeply towards conifers and go on the path down through them to a deer fence. Pass through the gate and on down to Glencanisp Lodge. Turn right and walk past the back of the house then past a block of garages on the right. Continue into woodland and down to the shore of a large loch, where you may see black-throated divers. Here the track becomes metalled.

3 At the end of the loch pass through a gateway to a parking area; this is the beginning of the public road along which you continue into Lochinver. Turn right and return along the seafront to your car.

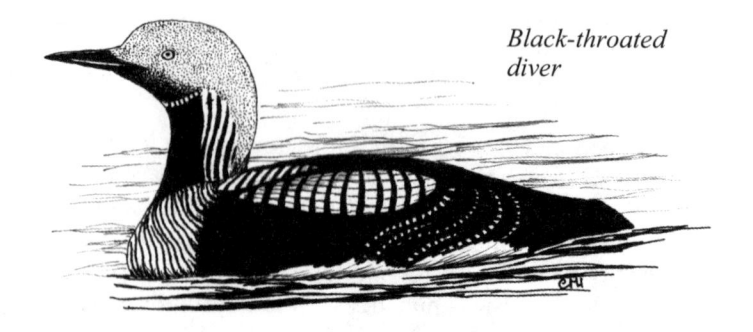

Black-throated diver

Practicals

Type of walk: The paths are good and quite distinct. There is some road walking at the end, which is mostly on a very minor road from Glencanisp Lodge. Through Lochinver there is a pavement.

Total distance: 4½ miles/7.4km

Time: 2–3 hours

Maps: OS Explorer 442/Landranger 15

38

Falls of Kirkaig and Fionn Loch

Park in the car park by the road bridge over the River Kirkaig, below Achins Book Shop and Café, grid reference 085193. Access this by driving south from Lochinver along a minor road, which goes left just before the new bridge over the Culag River. Continue through Strathan and Inverkirkaig to reach the bridge.

The **Falls of Kirkaig** are found on the boundary between Ross and Cromarty and Sutherland, beneath Suilven. The falls are 54ft/18m high and as the river drains a major system of lochs, there is always a good volume of water in them.

Fionn Loch, the white or fair loch, joins Loch Veyatie and together they extend almost to the A835 at Elphin. In order to climb Suilven from this side you have to make a wide detour round the west end of the loch.

Falls of Kirkaig

Suilven is the most iconic mountain in Sutherland, rearing up over the low gneiss countryside like some great sea-monster. The Vikings called it Sul-r (pillar) or Sul-fjall; Thomas Pennant in the 18th century called it 'the Sugar Loaf'. In fact from the side it can be seen to be a long narrow ridge, but this is hidden from its ends.

1. Cross the road from the car park, following a signpost to Falls of Kirkaig. Go through a kissing gate beside the main gate across the metalled access road on the right of the track to Achins. Listen for blackcaps and willow warblers in the bushes. Walk up the road until you reach a gate. Take a path which goes off right and runs along above a deer fence through birch and hazel woodland. Go through a deer gate and carry on along the delightful path to reach a vague junction and bear right. There is a notice here warning you of the dangers of the falls. Go on downhill along the lovely way, with primroses, violets, wood anemones, wood sorrel and bluebells below the trees in spring. Follow the path to the riverbank and stroll on beside it. Here in times of spate you may see salmon jumping the little falls.

2. Climb round a curve in the path, where a burn comes down, and then go on through great banks of gorse, coconut scented in the sun. Climb again, eventually to come out above the trees and gorse onto open moorland with the river now far below and a view of Cul Mor, Cul Beag and Stac Pollaidh to the south. Cross the level moorland with a brief glimpse of Suilven to the left, then at a path junction there is another warning sign about the dangers of climbing down the falls. Take the right branch and descend, with care, the path, a natural rocky staircase, rather eroded in places. Go down as far as you feel comfortable, although it is possible to get most of the way down. The view of the waterfall gets better all the way although you can see it quite well from high up. In certain conditions the pool at the bottom seethes with salmon, unable to jump the falls. Then start your return, which seems much easier than the descent.

Walk 38

3 At the path junction, turn right, skirting the higher cliffs above the gorge, and emerging into a more open area. Stroll the path as it moves close to the now calm river and continue to a cairn. The distinct path, left, is your way of return, but first carry on ahead until the river merges into Fionn Loch. The path is quite wet all round here and if the water is not too high it is more pleasant to walk on the exposed pebbly shore. Common sandpipers flit and call and you may well see a greenshank with its haunting cry, and possibly a dunlin. Enjoy the amazing view of Suilven across the water. Carry on round the shore, choosing the best way to avoid the wet areas, until the path turns up a small valley. At the top join another path and turn left. Cross the moor to reach your outward path. Turn right and retrace your steps to the car park, missing out the falls on the way back.

Common Sandpiper

Practicals

Type of walk: Good paths all the way although rather wet and boggy round Fionn Loch. The views across the loch to Suilven are magnificent. Care should be taken around the falls, especially with children.

Total distance: 7 miles/11.5km
Time: 4–5 hours
Maps: OS Explorer 442/Landranger 15

39a

The Traligill Caves

Park in the large car park at Inchnadamph, grid reference 251217. Access this by the A837 from Lochinver to Bonar Bridge.

The **Durness Limestone** is the oldest limestone in Britain but still the youngest rock in Assynt, a mere 500 million years old. It runs in a band from Durness in the north down to Loch Kishorn in the south, but reaches its thickest and biggest exposure at Inchnadamph. It affects the soils, which are much greener and more fertile wherever it outcrops.

Traligill Cave

132

The **cave system** to which these caves are connected is the most extensive in Scotland, running for many miles underground. Only experienced cavers should venture into it.

Two kilometres to the north of Inchnadamph the ruins of **Ardvreck Castle** stand on a peninsula in Loch Assynt (you can see it from the road). This castle is notorious as the place where the Marquis of Montrose, fleeing over the hills after defeat at Carbisdale, sought refuge and instead was taken prisoner and handed over to General Leslie by Neil MacLeod, the then chief of Assynt. Montrose was taken to Edinburgh and hanged. MacKenzie, Earl of Seaforth, took revenge, devastating Assynt and then holding it as his own land for 100 years.

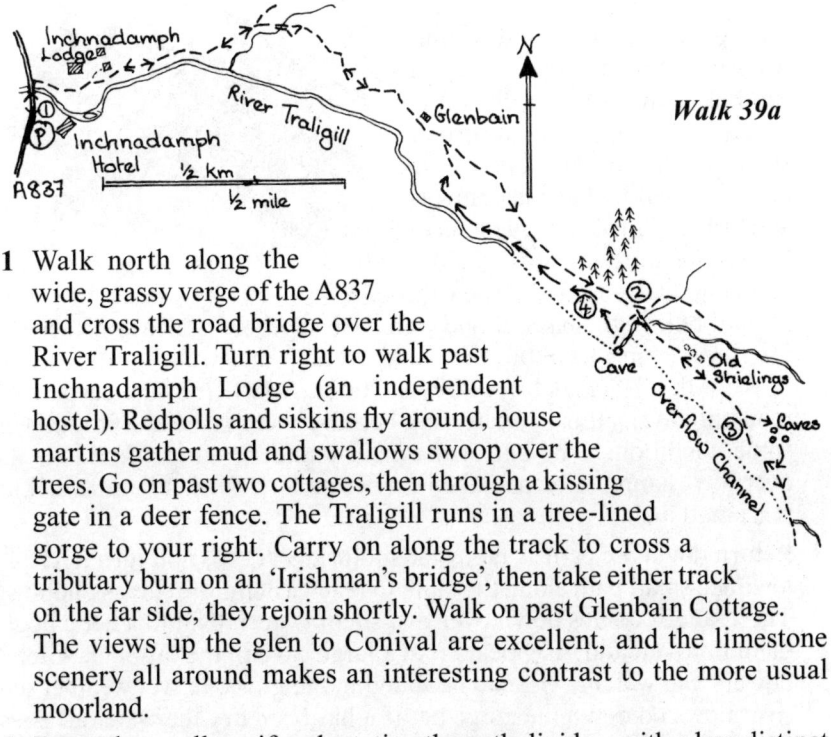

Walk 39a

1 Walk north along the wide, grassy verge of the A837 and cross the road bridge over the River Traligill. Turn right to walk past Inchnadamph Lodge (an independent hostel). Redpolls and siskins fly around, house martins gather mud and swallows swoop over the trees. Go on past two cottages, then through a kissing gate in a deer fence. The Traligill runs in a tree-lined gorge to your right. Carry on along the track to cross a tributary burn on an 'Irishman's bridge', then take either track on the far side, they rejoin shortly. Walk on past Glenbain Cottage. The views up the glen to Conival are excellent, and the limestone scenery all around makes an interesting contrast to the more usual moorland.

2 Beyond a small conifer plantation the path divides, with a less distinct branch going on up the ravine of the Traligill and the more obvious path going right. Follow this one down to a footbridge over the Traligill at which point there is a carved stone to mark the boundary of the National Nature Reserve. Climb up the far side onto a rocky limestone ridge. From now on, in May and June, you will find quantities of mountain

133

avens in the grass and on the rocks, as plentiful as daisies. There are also early purple orchids, yellow mountain saxifrage, alpine lady's mantle, and wild strawberries. Continue on the stalkers' path past the remains of an old shieling, on the left, to another fork in the path. Take the left branch towards the obvious cave in the rock ahead. You will want to spend some time here exploring. The first cave is the most dramatic, with a river, the Allt a'Bhealaich, rushing through the bottom and a small waterfall lit by the light through a sinkhole above. Ferns on the walls include the uncommon green spleenwort, among lots of the ordinary maidenhair spleenwort, and brittle bladder fern. The second cave is not quite so exciting, although you can clearly hear the river through a small hole at the base of one wall. The sinkhole is also spectacular. Carry on round to rejoin the stalkers' path and walk up the valley of the Allt a'Bhealaich for 220yds/200m. Apart from the carpets of mountain avens this is interesting because there is a waterfall, dry in some conditions. The burn runs mainly underground and this is its overflow channel. The path then carries on for a further ½ mile/0.7km to a small loch.

Mountain Avens

3 Return down the path as far as the footbridge. Cross and turn left, following a small path along the bank to reach a delightful grassy hollow. The Traligill comes down over two small waterfalls into a deep pool, then flows out and disappears into a large cave in the far bank. Globe flowers and water avens can be found in the grass. In wet weather the river flows on down the gorge but if it has been dry the water all goes underground here, leaving a dry river bed.

4 Go back up to the main path and past the plantation. Either retrace your steps down the track or cut off left again, winding through some lovely limestone pavement, to walk a narrow path above the dry gorge, with a fence to your right. At one point the river reappears only to go again almost immediately. Cross a rather boggy area and then at the end of a

field wall turn right through a gate gap in a fence. Walk up beside the wall to join a smooth grassy path. Turn left and walk out to rejoin the main track just before Glenbain Cottage. When you next see the river it is full of water.

Redpoll

Practicals

Type of walk: Interesting walk on good tracks and paths, with the possibility of a minor detour beside the often dry river. Care should be taken round the caves.

Total distance: 4 miles/6.5km, or 5½ miles/9km if you go on to the loch.

Time: 2–3 hours

Maps: OS Explorer 442/Landranger 15

39b

The Bone Caves

Park in the car park, signed for the bone caves, on the east side of the A837 about 2 miles/3.4km south of Inchnadamph, grid reference 253179.

The Bone Caves

The **Bone Caves**, in the base of a limestone cliff below Beinn an Fhuarain, were found to contain the bones of many animals such as brown bear, arctic fox, reindeer, lemming and lynx, known to have lived here after the last Ice Age but which have since been wiped out. It is thought that the caves may have been used as shelter by early hunter-gatherers living in this area. Hundreds of pairs of reindeer antlers were also found.

1. Walk out of the car park away from the road, through a kissing gate and follow the path to the left of an agricultural building. The path continues along the bank of the Allt nan Uamh (Burn of the Cave) past an attractive waterfall below a birch tree. Climb the bank beside the waterfall up a pitched path. From the highest point of the path look ahead to see a huge outcrop of limestone on the far side of the valley; this is your destination. Cross a burn on stepping stones and gradually descend into the valley again. A short distance further on a river suddenly emerges from a large spring called Fuaran Allt nan Uamh (the spring of the burn of the cave). It is quite amazing; there is no sign of a cave or slit in the rock, just a still, gravel-floored pool with a sizeable, rapid river flowing out of it. If you look very closely you can see where the water is welling up between the stones. The path goes round the head of the spring and continues up the valley.

2. After 1 mile/1.5km. the path forks. Take the right branch, which crosses the river. There is usually no water in the river this far up the valley; like the Traligill 2 miles/3.4km to the north this burn flows underground most of the time and only emerges above the surface after heavy or prolonged rain. The path, again pitched, climbs steeply up a narrow grassy spur on the far side, then contours and climbs again with steps in places to the caves. There are four, cut into the base of a limestone cliff at the top of a steep grassy bank, where you may see flowers like mountain avens, and mossy and yellow mountain saxifrages. The caves are deep and extensive and connect with the enormous cave network underlying this whole area. If you have a torch you can go a little way in, but only experienced cavers should explore it.

Walk 39b

3 From the fourth and last of the well-visited caves take a path which carries on ahead, slightly downwards at first but then contouring round the hillside. It is a good path although the drop on the left is very steep and may not appeal to people with no head for heights. Round a rocky buttress take the left branch and gradually descend to the valley, where the path makes a hairpin bend to the left (it actually joins a path going on through the valley but the continuation is quite vague). As you come back down the valley enjoy the view across to the base of the cliff and the caves seen clearly in context. Also look for buzzards and ravens which frequent this area. Rejoin your outward path at the fork where you crossed the dry river.

Mossy Saxifrage

Raven

Practicals

Type of walk: A fascinating short walk on good well-marked paths. The way up to the caves is easy underfoot but there is a very steep drop to the left, and the cave system itself is dangerous unless you are experienced. You may prefer to walk the loop the other way round to have a good view of the caves from a distance before seeing them in close-up.

Total distance: 3 miles/5km
Time: 2–3 hours
Maps: OS Explorer 442/Landranger 15

40

Canisp

Park in a large layby at the side of the A837, just beyond the north end of Loch Awe, about 2½ miles/4km north of Ledmore Junction, grid reference 250162

Canisp is a Corbett and at 2753 ft/847m is one of the higher mountains in the immediate area. It is a long ridge running from south-east to north-west along the southern side of Loch Assynt, but although in other company it would look quite dramatic, beside spectacular mountains like Suilven and Quinag it looks rather ordinary. However because of its isolated position it is a fine climb and affords fantastic views over Assynt and the other nearby hills.

Cam Loch and Canisp

Walk 40

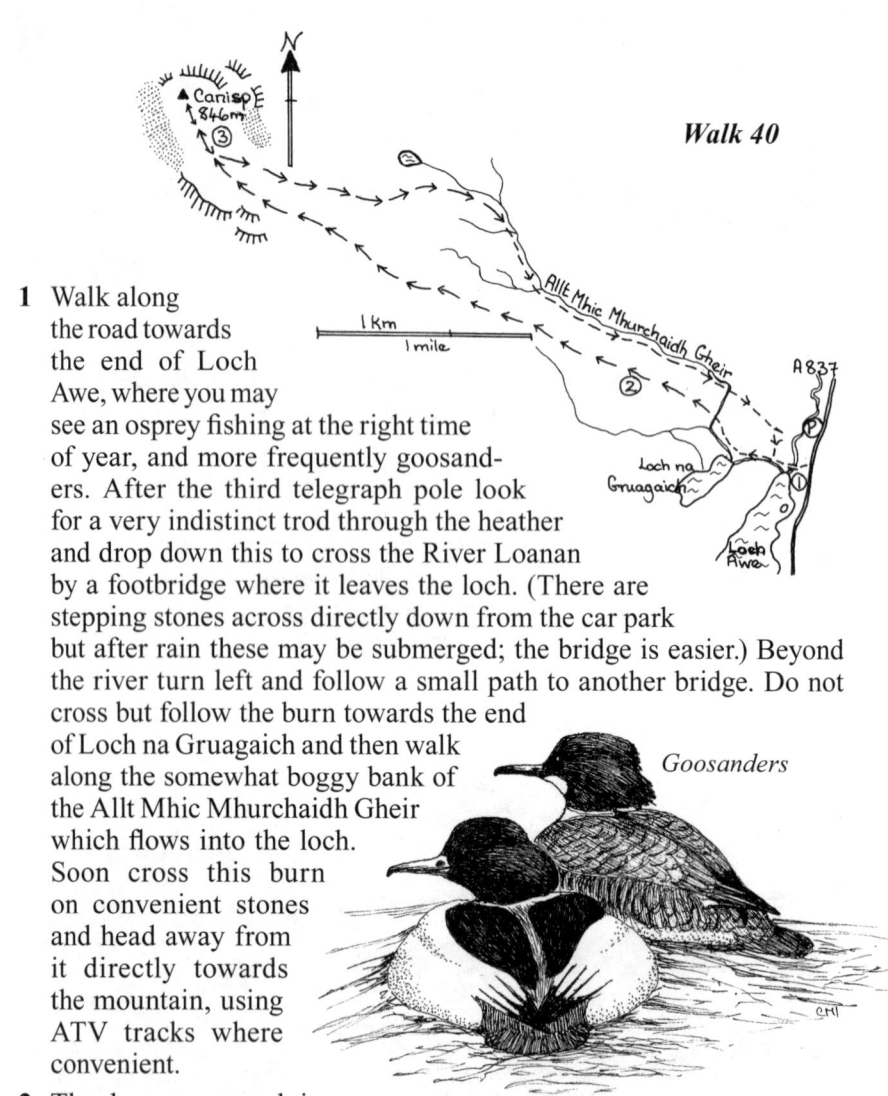

1 Walk along the road towards the end of Loch Awe, where you may see an osprey fishing at the right time of year, and more frequently goosanders. After the third telegraph pole look for a very indistinct trod through the heather and drop down this to cross the River Loanan by a footbridge where it leaves the loch. (There are stepping stones across directly down from the car park but after rain these may be submerged; the bridge is easier.) Beyond the river turn left and follow a small path to another bridge. Do not cross but follow the burn towards the end of Loch na Gruagaich and then walk along the somewhat boggy bank of the Allt Mhic Mhurchaidh Gheir which flows into the loch. Soon cross this burn on convenient stones and head away from it directly towards the mountain, using ATV tracks where convenient.

Goosanders

2 The boggy ground is soon left behind and the going becomes stony with frequent slabs of quartzite, which give enjoyable walking. Head for a cairn on a rise ahead, then continue straight up the broad stony south-east ridge. In clear weather the way is never in doubt. There is a steep final pull-up to the summit, where you are rewarded by a superb view. There is a stone shelter and various cairns, and at the time of writing there is a globe-shaped stone sculpture.

3 To return you can just retrace your steps directly. However for a change bear left after descending the short steep slope from the summit and walk down the shallow corrie on the north side of the hill. This is often relatively sheltered and can give a pleasant change on a windy day. Below you is a lochan tucked into the flank of the hill; make your way down towards the outflow from this and then follow the burn, the Allt Mhic Mhurchaidh Gheir, down, using a small intermittent path. It is a very attractive burn, full of pools and waterslides, and on a hot day can be very tempting. At the foot of the mountain the burn makes a right-angled bend and can be seen flowing into a short gorge. Cross on the corner, where stones and slabs make it easy, and follow a path across the boggy ground beyond. Climb a low hill at the far side and then leave the path and head right to come back down to the bridge (the path goes straight over the hill and leads to the stepping stones). Cross the bridge and return to the road.

Osprey

Practicals

Type of walk: This is a pleasant, relatively easy climb, although like all high mountains it must be treated with respect and can be a difficult proposition in winter. The paths are often indistinct or non-existent but in good weather the way is obvious. The lower ground is quite boggy and crossing the burn could be difficult if it has been very wet. Quartzite slabs can be slippery in wet weather. The views are splendid and make the whole excursion well worthwhile.

Total Distance: 8 miles/13km
Time: 7–8 hours
Maps: OS Explorer 442/Landranger 15

Walking Scotland Series
from Clan Books

MARY WELSH has already compiled walkers' guides to each of the areas listed: material for guides covering the remaining parts of Scotland is being gathered for publication in future volumes.

Titles published so far:

1. WALKING THE ISLE OF ARRAN
2. WALKING THE ISLE OF SKYE
3. WALKING WESTER ROSS
4. WALKING PERTHSHIRE
5. WALKING THE WESTERN ISLES
6. WALKING ORKNEY
7. WALKING SHETLAND
8. WALKING THE ISLES OF ISLAY, JURA AND COLONSAY
9. WALKING GLENFINNAN: THE ROAD TO THE ISLES
10. WALKING THE ISLES OF MULL, IONA, COLL AND TIREE
11. WALKING DUMFRIES AND GALLOWAY
12. WALKING ARGYLL AND BUTE
13. WALKING DEESIDE, DONSIDE AND ANGUS
14. WALKING THE TROSSACHS, LOCH LOMONDSIDE AND THE CAMPSIE FELLS
15. WALKING GLENCOE, LOCHABER AND THE GREAT GLEN
16. WALKING STRATHSPEY, MORAY, BANFF AND BUCHAN
17. WALKING AROUND LOCH NESS, THE BLACK ISLE AND EASTER ROSS
18. WALKING CAITHNESS AND SUTHERLAND

Books in this series can be ordered through booksellers anywhere.
In the event of difficulty write to
Clan Books, The Cross, DOUNE, FK16 6BE, Scotland.

For more details, visit the Clan Books website at
www.walkingscotlandseries.co.uk